*The* Ultimate Gift

# *The* Ultimate Gift

### Embracing the
### Joy of Eternal Love

## WILLIAM C. HAMMOND

**With a Foreword by Suzanne Giesemann**

Tasora
Minneapolis

Tasora Books
5120 Cedar Lake Road S
Minneapolis, MN 55416
(952) 345-4488
Distributed by Itasca Books

ISBN: 978-1-934690-78-9

Proceeds earned from the sale of this book will be donated to the Victoria K. Hammond Scholarship at the Kansas City Art Institute.

To my sister,

Clarissa H. Endicott

And in loving memory of her husband,

Thomas Hart Endicott

# A Message of Hope

It seems the light has gone out of your life.
The one you did care for most is gone.
There seems no reason now
To arise with the dawn.

You walk around in a daze
Wondering, "What's it all for,
If from my life has been taken
The one I most did adore?"

Just know that it's true:
'Tis better to know love as you had
Even though your heart breaks now
And you feel you'll go mad.

There are many who live
Who never know love like yours.
But in meeting your soul mate
You opened wide love's great doors.

Know that this love
While it's gone from you here,
Can never be taken
Though you shed many a tear.

She looks down on you now
And reaches out to your face
To wipe away your great sadness
And your spirit embrace.

Gone from your sight
But not from your heart . . .
You and your Victoria
Are never apart.

As close as your thoughts
She is there at your side.
For now in your memories
Your love does reside.

—Sanaya

This message was sent to me on August 17, 2011, via Suzanne Giesemann. Who is Sanaya? Suzanne explains: "Sanaya has told us that she is a collective consciousness of minds with both a feminine and masculine energy. This energy comes from a higher dimension than our own. When I bring through Sanaya's words, I am 'tapping in' to Higher Consciousness. I am allowing that Consciousness to express itself through my body: through my brain, through my vocal cords, my arms, my hands, and also through my pen. Sanaya would not need a name, except for our human need to put labels on things and place our experiences into well-defined boxes. Sanaya takes us outside the box into a dimension where we come face to face with our higher selves."

# *Foreword*

I am well acquainted with the searing pain of loss. When my beautiful stepdaughter Susan was killed by a lightning strike at age 27 along with her unborn baby, I didn't know how our family would bear the pain. It was a leap of faith that carried my husband Ty and me across the chasm of grief to land squarely in the presence of a gifted medium. The verifiable evidence that came through from our Susan forced me to change my limited beliefs about a greater reality and life beyond death.

Already a published author, I felt compelled to share in writing the reassuring message that death is merely a transition. When I approached my literary agent, Bill Hammond, with a proposed biography of a well-known, talented medium who had married a former Jesuit priest, he reacted with surprise. Certainly it was not the kind of subject matter he expected from an author whose background included twenty years as a U.S. Navy officer. It was that very background, however, that allowed him to trust my judgment and my manuscript.

When Bill secured me a contract with the esteemed publisher Hay House for my book *The Priest and the Medium*, I felt immense gratitude. I did not know how I could repay his gift of faith in representing me. Never did either of us imagine that within a few years I would repay him by presenting him the same gift that a medium had given to Ty and me.

I recall far too well the phone call from Bill in which he told me about the loss of his beloved wife, Victoria. I knew by that time that death is only a temporary separation from those we love, and I am not one to cry easily. But I also knew that he and his wife shared a depth of love that few couples achieve. I enjoy such a love with my husband, and I felt Bill's pain so intensely that upon setting down the telephone I sobbed.

I promised Bill that I would fly to Minneapolis to attend Victoria's memorial service. Those plans changed when Bill called me a while later to ask a special favor. He knew that my Susan's death had propelled me on a most unexpected spiritual journey. As a result, I had discovered the ability to see, hear, and sense those on the other side and was now working as a medium just like the woman Ty and I had visited. When Bill asked if I would be willing to give him a reading, I was honored to do so, but it would mean not attending the memorial service. I had only briefly met Victoria and I knew very little about her. I wanted all that I learned to come directly from Victoria's spirit and not from the things others might say in their tributes to her.

Bill understood and accepted my request to miss the memorial service. He then added a special wish of his own:

that I give him the reading on his birthday. I was more than
a bit nervous when that day arrived. Although by then I
had dedicated my life to perfecting my abilities, they were
still quite new. Just like searching for a cell phone signal in
unknown territory, there is no guarantee of a good connection in every reading.

I need not have worried.

When a bond of love exists as strong as that between Bill
and Victoria, the barrier between the physical and spirit
world dissolves far more easily. This was proven to us over
the course of three readings that were as close to a "phone
call from heaven" as any of the hundreds of readings I have
given. The ease with which Victoria communicated her
messages of love from beyond the veil astonished me. The
unmistakable evidence and reassurance that she presented
to Bill of her continued existence left him shaken to the
core. I know the feeling well.

It is earthshaking to hear from a loved one who has
passed that they are still with us. It changes everything. Yes,
we still miss their physical presence, but we know now that
we will see them again. To be able to provide this knowledge to a man who is now one of my dearest friends is—as
this book is so aptly entitled—the ultimate gift.

I am deeply humbled and awed by my ability to communicate with spirits and to pass on their messages to those
left behind. I connect with them most clearly when I am in
an expanded state of consciousness. It is for this reason that
I often forget most details of a reading when I return to the
more restricted state of awareness of normal human life. In
the process of reading the manuscript for this book, I found

myself stunned by the depth and clarity of evidence that Victoria communicated to Bill through me.

I deliberately maintain a state of emotional neutrality during a reading so as not to disrupt the flow of information. I lost that neutrality when reading this book. Bill has captured the emotion of his readings so clearly that in reliving them I cried just as I did when Bill told me of his wife's passing. This time my tears were tears of gratitude at being used as the conduit for Victoria's healing messages of love and comfort.

Just as I am grateful to Victoria for the clarity of her presence, I am grateful to Bill for sharing these most personal exchanges with those who will now benefit from hearing them. By including verbatim transcriptions of his readings, he allows you, the reader, to experience how life-changing evidential mediumship can be. The connection is real, and this gift of a book proves it. It provides irrefutable validation that life is eternal.

Thank you, Bill Hammond, for sharing Victoria's gift to you with the world, and thank you, Victoria, for showing us all that love never dies.

— Suzanne Giesemann

# Preface

On Sunday, May 1, 2011—the day my beloved wife died of cancer—my life came undone.

How could this have happened? How could my storybook marriage to such a lovely and loving woman have come to such an abrupt and cruel end? Some facts are indisputable. Victoria had kept an ominous medical condition hidden from me and our three sons, one of whom was a premed student at the University of Minnesota. She had lost weight, certainly. But she showed none of the typical signs of serious illness such as dark, sunken eyes; she had not lost her sense of decorum or humor; and until the final days before going to the hospital in an ambulance, she had maintained her normal daily schedule. Numerous appeals from her family for her to see a doctor and have her condition checked out fell on deaf ears. In her mind—as I was to discover during a hallowed day of grace shortly before her care was transferred from the oncology wing of Methodist Hospital in Minneapolis to its hospice services—the moment she accepted medical intervention, the life she loved and cherished would end. Instead, she wished to hang on to each day for as long as she was physically able to do so.

I knew from previous conversations starting even before our wedding day that she had no wish to undergo round after grueling round of chemotherapy and/or radiation, only to have her family watch helplessly as she wasted away. On that, we were of one mind. Her most devout wish now was for all of us to accept what had become the inevitable and allow her to slip quietly into the night.

To this day I do not know how long she suffered with that terrible secret growing inside her. Certainly it must have been many months, and during the last of those months the pain must have been excruciating—even though she declared to the hospital staff that she had rarely experienced any pain. Why did she accept such pain and do nothing to mitigate it? Part of the reason was denial and another part is profiled above. But there was more to it than that. Much more. To anyone who knew Victoria, the real answer lies in the heart and soul of a dear woman who would do—and did—everything humanly possible to spare her family the emotional and physical anguish she was enduring. It was her ultimate gift of love to those she loved so dearly.

The "day of grace" mentioned above was on Easter Saturday, April 23, 2011, four days before Victoria slipped into an irreversible coma and eight days before her death. In hospice parlance, that Saturday was Victoria's "rally day," a common phenomenon during which terminally ill patients act completely normal and even request favorite meals and beverages. Some patients even manage to dress themselves and try to leave the hospital or hospice to enjoy a day at home or in the outdoors. Victoria did not go that far—she would not have been able to, because by that time I was with her throughout the day and night—but for that entire day she was completely lucid and her skin glowed to an extent even the director of oncology at the hospital found astonishing. In short, Victoria looked every bit the beautiful young woman I had so proudly and joyously married nearly thirty-four years earlier.

We said much to each other that day. I finished reading *Have a Little Faith* to her and started reading *Heaven Is For Real*, and we discussed both books at some length. But it is the words of love we spoke to each other as the day progressed that are forever seared in my mind and etched on my heart. On several occasions I came close to breaking, but somehow, from somewhere in the depths of my being, I found the wherewithal to be strong. For her. No, *because* of her. Throughout that day she remained a paragon of calmness, grace, and serenity, no matter how sensitive or emotional the subject at hand. It was as though she had been visited by an angelic source and knew exactly what pain-free bliss awaited her on the other side. At no time during her three-week stay in the hospital did she display a hint of fear, despair, or regret.

By late afternoon of that Easter Saturday I could see she was tiring and needed to rest. I asked her if she would like me to continue reading *Heaven Is For Real* and she enthusiastically nodded her agreement. In a surge of hot emotion, I sat beside her on the hospital bed and took her hand in mine. Holding it to my heart, I looked deep into her eyes and said, my voice cracking, "Don't ever leave me, Dear-heart. Please God, don't *ever* leave me."

She smiled up at me, her expression a study in peace and sincerity. Giving my hand a gentle squeeze, she said, *sotto voce*, "I will never leave you, Dearheart, not ever. This I promise you; we will spend every minute of eternity together."

In the days, weeks, months, and years to follow I would receive irrefutable evidence—through a series of events, relationships, and synchronicities that I could not possibly have anticipated or imagined on that Easter Saturday— that this was a sacred promise my beloved Victoria intends to keep.

## Chapter 1

## Bill

While growing up on the rocky shores of Cape Ann, Massachusetts, I never considered myself a particularly religious
young man, although I certainly had the grooming and
grounding to become one. Service to God runs deep in the
ancestry of both sides of the Hammond family, and those
of my blood who prefer service to Man and Country have
often been driven by a higher mission of one sort or another.
Being so motivated had become a family trademark.

My father was among those who sought a different venue.
Although as a teenager he dreamed of playing catcher
for the Boston Red Sox, by the time he was preparing for
college and business school he had his eyes set resolutely
on Wall Street and investment banking. Mind you, in the
1950s and 1960s, investment banking was a far different
business than it is today. One could claim with a straight
face that it was an honest and honorable profession, not
quite akin to the priesthood, perhaps, but one rivaling
teaching or practicing medicine. So he did not entirely
break the family mold with his decision to rise up through

the ranks, first, of Lehman Brothers and then to the top of the pyramid at the great love of his life (aside from his family and fishing): White, Weld & Company, a prestigious and privately held international investment banking firm that was acquired by Merrill Lynch in 1974.

However, for all his worldly success (and "worldly" back then translated into a tiny fraction of what it would signify today to the Wolf of Wall Street), Dad lost sight neither of what truly matters in this world nor of who created this world. He and my mother—a genteel Bostonian lady who personified an unshakable belief in the existence of God and the promise of a joyous afterlife for those whom God deems worthy—attended church every Sunday without fail, barring sickness, an emergency, or some other inescapable contingency. In addition, for many years Dad served on the vestry of our church and also as a selectman for our hometown on Cape Ann, with the responsibility of managing the financial affairs of both organizations. He thus served God and Man in the ways he best understood and for which he was most qualified.

My parents' religious beliefs and convictions meant that my two older sisters and I were groomed to follow in their footsteps. As young children we attended not only church services on a weekly basis but also Sunday school. There we were introduced to the wonders of the Bible and to the image of a judicious God who, at some critical day in the future, would see to it that good people received their just reward in the glory of heaven, and that bad people—a category that most definitely included bad boys and girls—received their just punishment in a far less sublime environment. I admit to being somewhat shaken after several of those Sunday school classes, but that unfortunate response to religious instruction evaporated like summer dew after we returned home to my mother's delicious Sunday dinner, and Dad and I began planning an afternoon that often included a fishing trip, whatever the season. Nor did we normally discuss in the car or over dinner what we had learned in Sunday school that morning. To my parents, such follow-up analyses served no purpose. All that mattered was that we had attended class. What we might have gleaned from an hour of rigorous study and lecture was immaterial. It was simply assumed that what needed to sink in had, in fact, sunk in.

Did it? Well, it certainly did for my older sister, Diana. For several of her teenage years she seriously entertained the notion of becoming an Episcopal nun, a calling that my parents sought to dismiss from her heart and mind. There may have been more compelling reasons for their opposition, but I think my mother feared that by becoming a nun her daughter might forgo the joys of marriage and having children, while my father feared she would forgo the joys of a reasonable standard of living. Ultimately Diana settled on nursing and served on one long tour of duty as a hospice nurse at the nation's first hospice center in Branford, Connecticut. In her choice of career and her unselfish devotion to people in dire need, Di-Di was a Hammond to whom our ancestors would bestow a knowing nod of pride.

As for my other sister, Clarissa, well, not quite as much. Becoming a nun was not high on her list of preferred careers, and like most teenagers she seemed to have an

array of tricks up her sleeve to avoid church services altogether, especially after she received her driver's license. The
service we normally attended was at ten on Sunday morning, but there was a shorter service at eight. Each Sunday
morning Cris announced that she was off to attend the
eight o'clock service, ostensibly "to get it over with" as soon
as possible and thus have more time to pursue her personal
interests during the remainder of the day. Of course, Cris
rarely attended the eight o'clock service. Far more often
than not she drove to a local coffee shop and whiled away
the time drinking her favorite beverage while plotting her
next moves in her earthly pursuit of the Kingston Trio. (She
was their number one groupie.)

At approximately 9:30, while the rest of us were getting
ready to leave for church, her little blue Valiant station
wagon would appear in the driveway, after which, to everyone's amusement, she would proclaim that she had found
the service to be "very spiritual." (Just as her grandmother
did years later in Maine, after drifting off to sleep during
the sermon.) Our parents were not duped by her Sabbath
shenanigans, but there were no consequences for Cris. To
their mind, after a certain age, religion was not something
to be rammed down their children's throat. Doing so would
accomplish nothing and would in fact be counterproductive.
If any of us wanted to ensure our place in the lower regions
of the afterlife, well, that was our decision. As our father
was wont to say, "At some point every parent has to hand in
his or her exam papers and accept the grade earned."

If my sister Diana was on one end of the religious observation spectrum and my sister Cris was flirting with the

other, I was somewhere in between, but definitely leaning toward Cris. What defined, for me, a good church service was neither the liturgy nor the sermon—both of which, in my opinion, tended to be performed in a more or less perfunctory manner—but rather the music. Anyone who knows me well knows that I am completely tone deaf. Unlike my two sisters, I inherited not one measly music-related gene from either of my paternal grandparents, one of whom was an organist at Mount Holyoke College and the other a concert-quality pianist. To this day, when I attempt anything melodious, people clap their hands—over their ears. I am nonetheless highly susceptible to beautiful music: a violin concerto by Beethoven, for example; or a traditional Christmas carol sung by the choir at King's Chapel in Cambridge, England; or any song sung by Kate Wolf. If a church service included beautiful music, it became meaningful and memorable to me. If I was moved by Spirit, in church or elsewhere, it tended to be on a beach at dawn, at sea under sail, or through the human voice combined with calming musical instruments.

At the age of thirteen, in eighth grade, I was enrolled in a boarding school in Massachusetts located about an hour's drive from my hometown. The school was and remains affiliated with the Episcopal faith—although tolerant of all faiths—and features on its intimate 384-acre campus a most impressive Gothic-style chapel. That chapel inevitably became a focal point of daily student life because attendance was required every morning at eight, Monday through Saturday. (We had classes on Saturday morning.) On Sundays, each student had to attend the eleven o'clock service, but he (sadly, there was no "she" enrolled in the school until after I graduated) could attend either an eight o'clock morning service or a six o'clock eventide service. Being by nature a morning person, I usually attended the early service because, in Cris' parlance, I wanted to get it over with and look forward to a late afternoon game of stickball or touch football on the campus Circle while rubbing it in to my "sleep in" classmates as they trudged resentfully toward the Chapel at 5:45. I will confess, however, that there were times in the depths of winter when I looked forward to the evening service, especially when a favorite priest and faculty member sang the liturgy in one of the most melodious voices I have ever heard.

In college I fit well into a crowd of fellow students to whom a church service on Sunday was, at best, a distant afterthought. Like any college student, I engaged in numerous bull sessions in which we of the intellectual elite, our thoughts and bravado well oiled by a keg or two of beer, discussed how we would change the world by applying our collective genius to solving its manifold puzzles and problems. I don't recall any solutions emanating from these sessions, although I do recall withdrawing from the heat of battle whenever the subject of religious beliefs was raised.

I well remembered my father's frequent admonition to avoid any serious debate that involves either politics or religion. "You will never change anyone's mind on either of these subjects," he warned me, "no matter how hard you try or how compelling your arguments. People will continue to believe what they want to believe. All you will do is get people riled up and make them bitter and angry." Wise advice that I have tried to heed every day of my life.

Only when I returned home for vacation did I pursue any sort of religious routine, and that was done mostly to assure my parents that I had not yet joined the fallen. But for the duration of my college career and at the start of my professional career, when it came to religion, I was on automatic pilot. I sailed blithely past one navigational aid after another, oblivious to what specific course I was following or who might have control of the helm.

Many have said that the death of a beloved family member forces those left behind to confront the cosmic questions surrounding life and death that have haunted humankind since the dawn of existence. But that was not the case for my sisters and me. As children, we were protected by our parents from the "unseemliness" of death whenever a loved one passed on. Any questions we might have put to them about the soul and where it goes after death would have been answered just as they were by our Sunday school teachers: "The soul of a person is what survives death. Heaven is where the soul ascends, and heaven is a place far, far away, accessible only through prayer—and then only in a one-way conversation. It is not for us mortals to understand any of this in the way we understand how a car engine works. But it *is* for us mortals to accept all of this as God's will and God's plan for us. Salvation and redemption are based entirely on faith and a belief in God."

That conventional answer certainly contains strands of truth. But it was hardly a response that an inquisitive mind would let pass unchallenged. Of course, at that time I did not have an inquisitive mind when it came to matters of religion. I accepted as gospel truth that which I had been taught to believe and let it go at that. Why be concerned? After all, at the age of twenty I was going to live forever, right? Even if not, I still had years ahead to contemplate why I was here and what mission, if any, I served.

In the meantime I pursued the great loves of my life: literature and writing. As a "dime a dozen" history and English major at the University of North Carolina, I fantasized about someday becoming a world-famous novelist. I made my first stab at literary immortality a few years after graduation while living on the coast of Maine with my uncle, a former professor of English at Yale. After a year and a half I completed *For God and England*, a novel set during the Hundred Years' War and the reign of King Edward III. Although in completing this opus I learned a great deal about the mechanics of writing and the military-like discipline it demands, the novel was never published—much to the benefit of American letters.

With the sad yet crystal-clear realization (reinforced more than once by my father) that I was not going to live on royalty checks, I turned to the industry that wrote those royalty checks. After making the rounds of Boston-based book publishers, I was offered a job in Kansas City, Missouri, as a publisher's representative for Little, Brown & Company. The timing of my job-seeking could not have been more propitious. Little, Brown had recently opened three new sales territories, and Kansas City was the only one left when I telephoned the sales manager to request an interview.

I accepted the subsequent job offer without hesitation, unaware of the chain of interlocking events already set in motion during the weeks and months preceding that critical interview. Had I known about those events—more to the point, had I known then what was to follow in the years ahead as a direct result of them—I might have concluded that this interview had been divinely inspired by forces outside my control and the limits of my knowledge.

Whatever the inspiration, I had secured the job I had prayed for, representing one of the most prestigious book-publishing houses in the world in a seven-state territory that would be entirely my own. No other Little, Brown employee would cross its borders except for the sales manager who flew out to help me establish my retail and wholesale accounts.

With Fate smiling brightly upon me, in early January 1976 I boarded a TWA flight in Boston, bound for Kansas City.

# Chapter 2

## Victoria

If as a youth I landed somewhere near the middle of the religious observation spectrum, leaning toward my sister Cris on the left, I believe it is fair to say that Victoria Karel in her youth was positioned not far from me, but leaning toward my sister Diana on the right.

As she grew up amid the golden grain fields of America's Great Plains, religion played an increasingly important role in her life and the life of the town in which she lived. Many citizens of northeastern Nebraska, including the Karel family, are of Czech descent, and they take their religion seriously. In the 1960s the town of Howells, population 700, supported two large Catholic churches and a smaller Lutheran church. In addition to a public elementary school and high school, Howells also offered a private Catholic elementary school to its citizens, half the tuition for which was picked up by their parish.

Although the physical environs in which Victoria and I grew up were considerably different from each other, and our backgrounds were also dissimilar, when it came to religion and service to God and Man, there were several significant similarities between her father and mine. Lambert Karel—a successful businessman who sacrificed much to provide for his wife, son, and three daughters—was among the most popular citizens of Howells. For years he served as a commissioner of Colfax Country in Nebraska, just as my father had served as a selectman of my hometown in Massachusetts. And as my father had been, Mr. Karel (or "Dad" as I would come to call him—because I wanted to) was a pillar of his church and his community, serving as ad hoc adviser to the priest and vestry on a variety of matters, many of them involving finances. Skipping a Saturday evening or Sunday morning service was not his norm, although Mr. Karel was no Captain Bligh on his quarterdeck. He remained open to interpretations and flexibility. If, for example, his beloved Kissinki (Czech for "little kiss," his pet name for Victoria) happened to be just home from summer camp, well, the good Lord would understand if the family took a day off from spiritual concerns to spend time together.

As an aside, my father also employed the rationale of the "good Lord will understand," but normally he invoked it only when weather and sea conditions on a given Sunday morning were ideal for fishing and the striped bass or bluefish were running. Of course, as a chip off the old block when it came to fishing, I was a beneficiary of that benediction. And I really *do* believe that God would understand. Certainly his son would. Jesus was, after all, a fisherman—as my father often pointed out.

When Victoria was ready to enter elementary school, there was no question which school she would attend. For the next nine years (K-8) the Catholic private school was her academic domain. Her teachers in all grades were Catholic nuns, and students who have ever attended a Catholic school anywhere in the world ipso facto share a common bond cemented by the nuns' strict discipline. Such students know from long and hard experience that the least infraction of rules can inspire a snap of a ruler on the wrist or backside, and a more egregious offense can put one squarely on the path to eternal damnation.

From private elementary school Victoria matriculated to public high school despite the nuns' best efforts to convince her to attend a convent school in Omaha. (The nuns received "incentives" from the Church whenever they set a young lady on the pathway to becoming a novitiate.) From everything her family and friends have told me—and none of which came as a surprise to me—she cut quite a swath in Howells during her teenage years. She was head cheerleader for the Howells Bobcats while also participating in several sports, and she excelled in her studies and at the piano while also helping out her father in his business and volunteering as a nurse's assistant in a local hospital. And during all these years she kept faith with the Catholic Church, taking to heart its time-honored traditions such as observing the six annual holy days of obligation, paying homage to the Stations of the Cross, and eating only fish on Fridays. (This last dictate would turn out to be our mutual favorite: we enjoyed eating seafood on *any* day.) From all outward appearances she was a true believer, putting into practice what she had been taught in elementary school and what her parents and priests had inculcated in her from an early age. In sum, her life was one of unselfish sacrifice and good will toward others.

But if you were to think that this inherent goodness made Victoria a candidate for sainthood, you would be sorely mistaken. She was no angel, nor would she ever have wanted to be thought of as one—except perhaps by her three sons many years later. Victoria sported an impish streak that ran wide and deep and continuous, especially when she operated in cahoots with Pat Brodecky, her best friend growing up in Howells. The antics of these two are still legendary in Howells. In the eighth grade they "tee-peed" (draped rolls and rolls of toilet paper over) the town's new post office one summer night. On another evening they passed what many of the younger set of Howells considered a rite of passage. They snuck off to the outskirts of town where the main transformer was located, threw the switch that turned off electricity everywhere in sight, and then ran, giggling, into a glade of woods to hide and watch chaos erupt. When they were experiencing the inevitable "boy problems" of teenage girls, Victoria knew just the right remedy. She "borrowed" the keys to her father's grocery store, and she and Pat snuck inside, removed a large Sarah Lee chocolate cake from a refrigerated display case in the bakery section, and took it to the dark quiet of the public tennis courts and drowned their sorrows in chocolate delight, leaving no a crumb behind as evidence of the crime of breaking and entering. (Well, perhaps just entering; they had a key, after all, and the only thing broken was their hearts.).

Even Victoria's summertime experiences at Camp

Kiwanis did not temper the playful mischief that was always such an endearing part of her personality. The week-long camp was a highlight of each summer for her and Pat, and how the two of them managed to survive that week and a subsequent week in summer religious education without being sent home early remains a mystery even to this day to those in the know.

Mind you, Victoria did not relate these or similar stories to me when we were dating. Nor did she tell me of them at any time during our blissful thirty-four-year marriage. It was not her way to talk about herself, especially when it involved those transformative early years of her life. Had she not predeceased me, I would never have known about any of them. I realize that statement may seem incongruous, but trust me, it will assume significant meaning and clarity in later chapters.

So the conclusion I reach is that while Victoria was certainly a good and loyal Catholic, she was an even better and more loyal daughter. She believed in the tenets of the Church because her parents believed them, her friends and neighbors believed them, and she had been taught to believe them. And she took those teachings to heart. Throughout the thirty-five years I knew her, I never heard her lie unless it was for a good purpose, and I never heard her use foul language or take the name of the Lord in vain. And I mean *never*. Not once. And she was honest to the core. I don't know what her father said to her when she proactively confessed to taking the chocolate cake from his store, but I imagine it went something like this: "Kissinki, if you want a cake or anything else from me, you just have to ask me for it. You know that I will always give it to you. In fact, here's ten dollars toward your next purchase." He couldn't punish his beloved daughter, no matter what she did. But the point is, he never needed to, no matter what she did.

Her father was not alone in forgiving Victoria for her various pranks and misdeeds. Everyone did. Whenever she and Pat were caught together with their hands in the proverbial cookie jar, and it didn't matter who caught them, the justice meted out was rarely equitable. As Pat recently told me, "Vicki was always sent home with nothing more than a pat on the head, as though she was somehow immune from admonishment or punishment. I was always the one who got whacked." Surprisingly, Victoria's peers did not ostracize her as a result. If anything, they admired her ability to avert bad consequences for harmless pranks and capers.

Of course, Victoria's knowledge of the history of the Catholic Church—especially those chapters that contradict the presumed ethical purity and inviolability of the pope and his priestly flock—was circumscribed. Such troubling material was not taught in Catholic elementary school or in high school, or even in college. Her faith was a blind faith, as it was for me—as it is for most people. Children and teenagers seldom question what is proclaimed in the name of God by those supposedly anointed by Him. It is accepted without reservation and without debate. To my knowledge, only Judaism encourages such debate. Every Jewish congregant has the sacred duty to constantly challenge the status quo and ask *why* things are done as they are, to be always on the lookout for a better way to enhance their spirituality and relationship with God. But that approach is not the norm in Christian faiths.

In college at the University of Nebraska in Lincoln, Victoria tended to shy away from intellectual debates about religion or other cosmic issues, just as I did. She saw no point in them. Instead, she devoted her time to her studies and her sorority, Alpha Delta Pi, where she thrived and to which she remained committed her entire life. And, of course, in the fall she attended every football game she could to cheer on the Cornhuskers in pursuit of national championships under the tutelage of legendary coach Bob Devaney.

In college she also pursued a long-held interest for art—not the study of it, the creation of it. People in Howells who knew her while she was growing up, including the nuns in elementary school, often commented on the God-given talent she exhibited in any drawing she fashioned, whether with pencil, chalk, or brush. In those early years the seeds were sown for a lifelong passion. Problem was, the University of Nebraska, while certainly a world-class institution, had limited resources and opportunities for students who wanted to hone their artistic skills. Her advisers told her that if she wanted to realize her full potential as an artist, she would need to abandon her pursuit of liberal arts and attend a school of art. The closest such institution to Howells, Nebraska, was the Kansas City Art Institute, which also happens to be one of the premier schools of art in the world.

What their beloved Kissinki desired, her parents struggled hard to make reality. So it was through their understanding and benefice that Victoria was able to take the plunge. With hardly a look back, she left her many friends and academic achievements at the University of Nebraska to pursue her dream of creating art. In late summer of 1969 she packed up her pale yellow Karman Ghia and headed south from Omaha along Highway 29, bound for Kansas City.

*Chapter 3*

*Love & Marriage*

I met Victoria on Labor Day 1976. We had a number of mutual friends who were involved in the broad-based publishing industry in Kansas City, and they were gathering for a beach party at a man-made lake not far away. Victoria was someone else's date—a fellow named Peter—and I was accompanied by a young woman named Sue Sheila who worked at a local bookstore. By sheer coincidence (if you believe in such things; I tend not to), Peter and Victoria were assigned to my car for the ride out to the lake.

When we neared our destination we stopped at a 7-11 and Peter and Sue Sheila hopped out of the car to purchase drinks, ice, and whatnot. During those first few minutes I had alone with Victoria, I heard a little of her story. She had graduated from the Kansas City Art Institute three years earlier, and after a stint teaching art at Penn Valley Community College was currently employed by the Kansas City office of the Landmarks Commission, researching the boyhood home of Walt Disney for inclusion in the National Register of Historic Places. Like legions of artists, musicians, and writers before her, she had learned one of life's bitter lessons; namely, that a God-given gift of artistic talent does not always translate into an earthly paycheck that can sustain a human being, no matter how righteous he or she might be. To Victoria, the Landmarks Commission seemed a viable and worthy alternative to the practice of art—and to the teaching of art to students who all too often were looking for an easy grade and lacked the passion and commitment of a true practitioner.

To say I was smitten by Victoria during that beach party would be a pathetic understatement. Although she was a strikingly beautiful young woman by anyone's standards, what drew me inexorably to her was her smile. It lit up her face and everything around her, including my heart. To me, she was the only person on that beach and the only reason to be there, and as the afternoon progressed I increasingly had the impression that she was experiencing the same sorts of emotion. So did Peter. Suffice it to say that on the drive back to Kansas City he made sure that he and Victoria rode in someone else's car.

What happened next is chronicled in a recently published book titled *Victoria: A Love Story*. To summarize, a year later, at six o'clock on September 24, 1977, Victoria and I were joined in holy matrimony in a Kansas City church. The formal, garland-bedecked ceremony is as unforgettable to me as the day itself: resplendent with a cerulean blue sky, a warm yellow sun, and the soft, appealing colors of early autumn. After a storybook honeymoon in the U.S. Virgin Islands, we settled for two years in Virginia, first in McLean and then in Alexandria. A job promotion then took us from Old Dixie to New England. After living for two years in Boston, we moved to the picturesque seaside town of Hingham on Boston's South Shore where we started raising our sons. In 1995, following receipt of a lucrative job offer in Minnesota, the Hammond family, now numbering five members, looked westward to Minneapolis.

⌐

How can I capture in a few pages the import of thirty-four years of wedded bliss to a woman who was everything a wife, mother, friend, and lover could possibly be—and to whom I owe an eternity of gratitude? It is an impossible task whatever my abilities as a writer. The good news is that I don't have to do that. The mission of this book is not to convince anyone that Victoria and I fashioned a marriage for the ages. Many couples believe, and rightfully so, that they too bask in that same redemptive glow of God's blessing. Rather, the mission of this book is to convince everyone that my life-defining relationship with Victoria did not end on May 1, 2011, the day she passed on from cancer. Death did no "do us part"—a phrase, incidentally, that we chose to eliminate from our wedding vows because we didn't believe it then and I certainly do not believe it now. Each day of my life, Victoria lives on in and around me in spirit form, as vibrant and loving and supportive of me and our three sons as she always was in physical form.

Here is the key message: If my dearly departed wife lives on in this way, so do your loved ones—all of them.

I will present irrefutable evidence that this is true. For the moment, please indulge me as I offer several additional glimpses into my relationship with Victoria. They will make what follows in later chapters more meaningful to you.

⌒

During the entirety of our thirty-four-year marriage, religion played a central role in our life together. In the early years, when we moved from Kansas City to Washington and from there on to Boston, we attended a number of different churches of various Christian faiths. We didn't much care which faith because we didn't believe that God puts much stock in such matters. In our view, no religion has it all right and no religion has it all wrong. Whatever our core beliefs, we are all worshiping and giving thanks to the Source, or Great Sprit, or whatever name one chooses to apply to God. We are all on an equal footing and of one mind with that Supreme Power of the Universe. That is a common thread running through all religions, and one that helps tie them all together.

In particular, we saw little difference between Catholicism and Episcopalianism, especially considering that what prompted King Henry VIII to sever heavenly ties with the pope in Rome—and thus establish the Anglican Church in Great Britain, the mother of the Episcopal Church in the United States—was his very earthly lust for Anne Boleyn. That so many millions of innocent people have been killed through the ages in the name of "the one true religion" must make God weep.

It was not until we moved to Hingham that we became members of a church. Our decision to join St. John's Episcopal Church was motivated by practical as well as spiritual considerations. Many of the people we had befriended on the South Shore were members of that church, and it had attached to it a highly coveted nursery school that we hoped our children would someday attend. (In fact, all three sons did.) Plus, it was a beautiful church with a full choir that sang in perfect harmony with our hearts. Most important to us, however, was the excellence of the clergy, in particular the Reverend Robert Edson, who is now retired and who to this day remains a close friend of my family.

After fourteen years of living in Hingham we moved to Minneapolis. Soon after settling in a western suburb of the city, we found another church home at St. Stephen's in Edina. We were drawn to the church initially by the recommendation of Father Robert, who had grown up with the St. Stephen's youth minister in the same New York town. ("Everyone loves Gary Dietz," Robert told us just before our move, "from parents on down to the tiniest tot.") As it turned out, Gary lived up to his billing in every sense of the word, as did every other member of the clergy. One in particular, the Reverend Graham Fenton, is one of the kindest and holiest individuals I have ever known. He too remains a close friend.

As a family we attended church every Sunday and became involved in church activities on other days of the week. Our two older sons were having a difficult time adjusting to the move from Massachusetts to Minnesota, and the open arms of St. Stephen's welcoming us into the church family did much to make the transition easier and quicker. Our oldest son in particular became heavily involved in the youth program and today regards Gary Dietz, now retired, as his mentor and one of his best friends.

Each evening, regardless of what might still be on the agenda, we sat down as a family at the kitchen or dining room table to give thanks to God for the blessings of the day. Victoria and I had both grown up following the daily ritual of saying grace, and she insisted on its continuance in our family. On this matter she held considerable sway over our strapping sons, because heaped before them on the table each evening was a feast for sore eyes and hungry stomachs, and no one was allowed to dig in until five seconds has elapsed after the "Amen." Victoria was a master chef, and there was nothing she enjoyed more than cooking for her boys—me included. In this and every activity in which she participated, Victoria was a perfectionist's perfectionist.

As much as she was a perfectionist, Victoria was also a traditionalist. What appealed to her were the classics: Big Band music, ballroom dancing, gentlemanly manners, that sort of thing. It was no different when it came to preparing meals, especially during the holidays. She insisted on having traditional foods and side dishes on the Thanksgiving and Christmas table, whether or not they were consumed. For example, when our eldest son could sit at the table with us, Victoria had a server of brown gravy there. It was what she had grown up with (as had I), and she wanted her family to have it on such momentous occasions as well.

When our sons were young, they consumed massive quantities of the brown stuff. They poured it liberally over their turkey, mashed potatoes, and stuffing, and drowned their vegetables as well. As they aged into their teenage years, however, and became more body conscious, they consumed less and less of the gravy until the inevitable

Thanksgiving came when they refrained altogether. Nevertheless, for each and every holiday feast after that, Victoria
placed the white porcelain gravy server on the middle of
the table in honor of its long tradition in our homes. Inevitably it became a standing joke within the family, and we all
looked forward (well, Victoria and I did) to another round
of good-natured "brown gravy" jokes and stories at the
holiday dinner table.

⌒

During the early years of our marriage especially, before we
started having children, we took great joy in pursuing what
more staid adults might consider to be "childish" activities.
For example, on one birthday Victoria presented me with a
model wooden sailboat complete with mainsail and jib. We
sailed the little boat on Accord Pond in Hingham or on a
man-made pond on the village green in the neighboring
town of Cohasset. And we took such delight in doing it.
On another occasion I gave Victoria a gift of a kite, which
we often flew on a Delaware beach, or later, on a beach
on Cape Cod or Nantucket. Taking delight in such simple
pleasures was symptomatic to us—and to many couples—of
being young at heart and in love.

One of our favorite activities was traveling. It didn't need
to be to an exotic locale. Just being in our little Ghia on a
Saturday morning with a cup of Dunkin' Donuts coffee in
hand and on the road to somewhere was a joy we shared
from the earliest days of our relationship. We did learn a
lesson early on, however, about how to select a place to stay
the night if a sleepover was on the agenda.

The summer before our first son was born Victoria and I went on a five-day road trip that included two nights in Montauk on the eastern tip of Long Island. We had booked a room at a local motel, which, to protect the guilty, I will call The Highlands. The brochure we had received in the mail made the motel look ideal, but of course this was before the introduction of the Internet and social media and online customer reviews. Such cost-cutting websites as kayak.com and hotels.com did not yet exist, and we were on a tight budget. The cost of a room at The Highlands, in relation to its advertised amenities, seemed more than reasonable.

It is said that one generally gets what one pays for, and this place proved no exception to that time-honored platitude. When we arrived late in the evening after a long journey by road and ferry, we checked into a room that was lean, mean, and unclean—and worse: it exuded an unpleasant aroma that suggested it was available to rent by the hour. Too exhausted to search elsewhere, and having already paid for one night's stay, that night we lay supine on top of the bed, fully clothed, fearful that the "Highlands monster," as Victoria labeled it, would materialize from under the bed and have at us. We could not wait to check out the next morning and seek lodgings more accommodating for a young couple deeply in love.

From that day forward we resolved never again to travel anywhere overnight unless we could stay in relative comfort. No more Highlands monsters for us, thank you very much, although for many years to come we joked about that wretched beast whenever we made reservations at *any* hotel or motel.

⌒

Victoria and I began another ritual soon after we moved into our home in Minneapolis and installed in our living room a gas fire that we could flick on with a switch located near the hearth. Unless one of us was away at the time, at six o'clock each evening we sat together by the fire, Victoria with a glass of white wine in her hand and me with a glass of scotch or vodka in mine, and discussed every topic imaginable—past, present, and future. As our family grew older and the demands of daily living became ever more challenging, this time together became ever more vital to us. It was *our* sanctuary, *our* time together as husband and wife, as intimate in its own way as those more physical intimacies we shared upstairs in our bedroom. Weather conditions outside mattered not a fig. During the heat and humidity of July and August, Victoria cranked up the air conditioner at five o'clock, to the degree that by six the warmth cast off by the gas fire felt pretty darn good. And there we would sit, as happy as two clams in the sand at high tide (as our sons often remarked), until jungle drums erupting upstairs signaled a mounting impatience for dinner.

⌒

When at the dawn of 2008 we entered our thirty-first year of marriage, we had every reason to be both grateful and optimistic. Our three sons were doing well and doing good work. I was self-employed as a business consultant and earning a more than decent living. Victoria was fulfilled as a woman and mother. Our love had expanded to fill an ocean, and we had many close friends who cared about us. And the housing and financial markets were continuing to burgeon, sailing blithely and confidently into uncharted waters, and thus ensuring our financial security in the years ahead. As we neared the end of the first decade of the twenty-first century, it seemed, for us, as though everything within reason was within reach. We had every reason to believe that the good times would roll on, and that whatever might come at us in the future would bring round after round of blessings and bounty, just as it had done in the past.

But as an author client of mine once wrote, "The only constant in life is change." In 2008 change was in the wind, and for us it came in the form of a Force 5 hurricane followed by swift and overwhelming devastation by an F6 tornado, neither of which we could possibly have foreseen or sought shelter from. The life we so cherished and strove to live to the fullest was under siege, and was soon to come crashing down on top of us.

# Chapter 4

## A World Turned Upside Down

Imagine a row of dominoes standing an inch or so apart from each other, perhaps in intricate patterns of arcs, circles, and straight lines stretching out over a wide area. Now imagine flicking your finger against the first domino. It falls over and hits the second domino, which strikes the third domino, and so on down the line until all five or fifty or five hundred ebony tiles have collapsed onto the floor. This imagery perhaps best symbolizes the misfortunes of my family beginning in 2008.

The first domino to fall was my vision. In the summer of 2008 I had two cataract operations spaced two weeks apart. Of all such procedures performed, 98 percent go without a hitch; as mine did, for a while. For several unforgettable months I had better than 20/20 vision in both eyes for the first time in my life. Ultimately, however, I was to fall within the unfortunate 2 percent. In November, during a business meeting, I began noticing black dots, hundreds of them, in my left eye's field of vision. After we had a quick consultation with my ophthalmologist, Victoria drove me to the Phillips Eye Institute in Minneapolis where I underwent emergency surgery for a severely torn retina. The outcome of that surgery was a significant loss of vision in that eye.

Despite that setback I still had nearly perfect vision in my right eye. So life went on, and I was able to continue my work as a business consultant for four different publishing entities, the most significant of which was IDC (International Diabetes Center) Publishing located within the Park Nicollet Heath Services complex in Minneapolis. That interval of sustained vision, however, proved ephemeral. In February 2009 I experienced the familiar white flashes in my right eye, and the next day the hundreds of black dots again intruded upon my vision. This circumstance entailed another operation at Phillips and an equal loss of vision in both eyes.

The row of dominoes now began to fall rapidly, as if up to this point it had simply been gathering momentum, waiting for the optimal moment to unleash its full fury. The original publisher of my projected six-book seafaring series closed its doors just six weeks before my second novel in the series was to be released (every author's worst nightmare). Meanwhile, the housing markets had collapsed, savaging the market value of our Minneapolis home. At the same time the financial markets collapsed, followed by a severe recession that sent the book-publishing industry reeling. Within a two-month period, all four of my consulting clients responded to the sharp decline in revenue and profits by circling the wagons and backsliding to survival mode. Park Nicollet took it a step further. With projected bottom-line results lagging to a point of no return, senior management made the understandable decision to no longer invest in any business that did not represent a core competency of the organization, whether or not that business was profitable (IDC Publishing was). That decision led to the shutdown of IDC Publishing and the layoff of its twenty-four full-time employees and its acting publisher, me.

With all four of my business clients now former clients, my earned income declined from a comfortable six figures to zero in a relatively few weeks. Of course, the considerable overhead and other expenses tied to this income stream did not disappear along with it. Those expenses remained, and the only way to address than was to dip heavily into savings and to sell investments. My father, a former Wall Street investment banker of some standing, would not have approved of selling investments after their value had been skewered. "Sit tight, don't panic, and wait for that market to rebound," was his time-honored and oft-heard advice, and of course he was right. But then, Victoria and I did not approve of what we were doing either. We simply saw no alternative. We had to weather the storm and care for our children as best we could under the circumstances.

So there we were at the close of 2010 with no earned income and, because of my poor vision, no realistic prospects of replenishing our accounts anytime soon. No longer able to drive outside of our immediate neighborhood or work on an Excel spreadsheet, I had to somehow reinvent myself and seek a new line of work I could do from home. Victoria, meanwhile, began scanning "help wanted" advertisements. To the extent they were able, our three sons helped out with odd jobs as they continued on with their university studies.

When disaster strikes a marriage, one of two things can happen. Either the husband and wife play a "blame game" that ultimately destroys the marriage, or the marriage grows as a result and becomes stronger than ever. To say that I was/am blessed in marriage is the understatement of the millennium. While Victoria was many things to me, she was above all else the giver of peace. Just being in her presence enabled me to meet any curveball or screwball that Fate might hurl at us on any given day. Night after night we sat together by the fire in our living room to discuss what we would do next and how we might best do it. Even our decision to stop paying a crushing monthly mortgage and property tax bill—and thus put our house into default—was done with equanimity and a strong dose of pragmatism. We even offered a toast to the wonderful memories our home had provided us and our sons. (As a footnote, through some legal maneuvering my family was able to remain in the house for nearly four years after going into default.)

Often, late at night, lying in bed and staring up at the ceiling, I asked myself how on earth I could survive this personal version of a holocaust without the love and support of the dear woman lying close beside me. Without her, I was nothing. With her, I was everything. Sadly, I was soon forced to answer my own question. What was about to happen trivialized everything that had preceded it and made a mockery of what I had heretofore considered to be "bad times."

⌒

In the preface to this book I chronicle some of what transpired after that terrible day of April 12, 2011, when Victoria was rushed to Methodist Hospital to receive a dire diagnosis of stage 4 colon cancer. She put up a brave and utterly unselfish front for so long, but after the die was finally cast by the arrival of the ambulance at our home, her health deteriorated rapidly. While in the hospital—first as a patient in the cancer ward and then as a hospice patient—she refused to eat anything, despite the urgings of the hospital staff. All she would ingest were sips of water and slivers of ice. She wanted to die, not because she wanted to leave her family but because she wanted to spare us her suffering.

In the preface I also refer to the "rally day" she experienced on Easter Saturday. That is indeed a day I will never forget. Later that morning, after our three sons had left her hospital room after what would prove to be our last interactive visit as a family unit—a visit I had to excuse myself from at one point to place a call to the Minnesota Cremation Society to arrange an early Monday morning meeting—I asked Victoria if she would like to rest for a while. When she smiled at me and said no, I drew a deep breath and resolved to broach subjects I had no desire to consider—then or ever.

"Dearheart," I said, using the pet name we had called each other since before our wedding day, "there are things we have never discussed that we should have discussed, a long time ago."

Her eyes held mine, and she nodded.

"We need to discuss them now," I said quietly.

Again she nodded, willing me to continue.

"Do you understand that I am putting you into hospice care starting Monday? I will call your brother and sisters tomorrow. But the decision is made."

I was well aware that this what Victoria wanted. We had discussed what we would do in such an eventuality even before we were married. Several days earlier, one of her doctors had recommended transferring her into what he referred to as a rehab center, where she might continue to show improvement after a period of chemotherapy and rehabilitation. At first encouraged by his prognosis, I had a swift change of heart the next morning when another of her doctors—a woman I trusted implicitly—confirmed what I feared most, that the "rehab center" was nothing more than a nursing home in which Victoria would receive minimal medical care. The real issue was that the hospital believed it could no longer offer my wife any further valid treatment, and therefore wanted to free up her private room. As a patient in the hospital-based hospice center, however, she could stay in the room she was in as long as she didn't show significant improvement—in which case she would be transferred out.

She squeezed my hand. "Thank you," she said in a surprisingly firm voice. "That was the right decision."

I kissed her on her forehead and tucked a stray strand of hair behind her ear. Looking at her lying there looking up at me with such trust and gratitude nearly shattered my resolve to remain strong for her. Her skin glowed and her face exhibited none of the manifestations normally associated with imminent death by cancer. We said what we needed to say to each other, and then I paused.

"Now for the last and hardest question," I said at length, struggling for composure. "I have to ask you: where do you want to be buried?"

"Next to you," she said without hesitation.

I swallowed hard. "That, my love, is a given," I choked. "But where? Do you have a preference?"

"No," she said calmly. "You decide for us."

I nodded and averted my gaze to hide the tears welling in my eyes.

When I felt her squeeze my hand, I returned my gaze to hers. To my utter stupefaction she was smiling at me and giving me that look of hers that had warmed my heart on countless occasions during our marriage. It was an expression of pure love.

"Dearheart," she soothed, "it will be all right. I *promise* you, it will be all right. We have an eternity to spend together."

"Dear God," I managed. "*I'm* the one who should be comforting *you*. I should be telling *you* that."

She just lay there, smiling up at me.

I took her hand in both of mine and gazed deep within her. "I don't know how to live without you, Dearheart," I said, despite myself, for those words, as if on cue, unleashed a flow of tears. "I don't *want* to live without you. I want to go with you."

"You can't," she said softly. "Not just yet. You must remain here for our sons. They will need you now more than ever."

"Yes," I said, because there was nothing else to say to that statement. I held up my left hand. "This I pledge to you, Dearheart," I vowed from the heart, my voice shaking. "I will never, *never* take off my wedding ring."

Victoria didn't blink. "Someone will have to cut your finger off to get it," she said, referring to a vow we had made to each other on our wedding night. That she had remembered the exact words of my response to that vow drove deep into the very core of my being. As if it were the most natural thing in the world to do, I lay down on the bed beside her, draped my right arm gently across her chest, and held her close to me until a nurse came into the room and separated us.

The next day, Easter Sunday, the rally day was over and Victoria reverted to what had become a daily routine of drifting in and out of sleep as her body continued to shut down. Even when she was awake, she was never again fully alert. On the following Thursday morning, just before she slipped into an irreversible coma, I said my last words to her.

The evening before, I had been sent home by Victoria's primary doctor to get some rest because I hadn't had much sleep in recent days. Early the next morning, when I first appeared on the oncology-hospice wing on the fourth floor of Methodist Hospital, I was met by a nurse who during the previous weeks had become a friend to Victoria and our entire family.

"Bill," she said, running up to me, "I'm so relieved you are here. I called your home a few minutes ago. Your wife is slipping into a coma. There's not much time, only enough time for you to say good-bye to her."

That I could not do. I could not and would not say good-bye to the person I loved more than my own life and who had defined my life for thirty-five years. Instead I walked into her room and sat down on the bed beside where she lay, seemingly in a deep sleep with her hands clasped loosely upon her stomach. Her chest rose and fell sporadically, as her breathing came in irregular intervals.

"Dearheart?" I said softly.

No response.

"Dearheart?" I said in a louder voice.

Her eyes fluttered open. When she saw me, she gave me a faint smile.

"Dearheart," I said to her gently, "The nurse tells me you are going into a coma."

She nodded weakly.

I placed my hand over hers and stared for the last time into her beautiful hazel green eyes.

"I love you with all my heart," I said with every ounce of conviction and love my mind, body, and spirit could muster. It was a phrase we had shared so often during so many tender moments between us.

She had hardly the strength to speak, but was able to mumble and mouth the words "I love you with all my heart" back to me.

Minutes later she slipped away. Four days later, at 11:17 on Sunday night, May 1, she died.

At that instant a large part of me died with her and my world went dark.

*Chapter 5*

*A Messenger of Hope*

I was first introduced to Suzanne Giesemann on a frigid morning in early January 2007 when a package arrived at my small literary agency in the Hyatt Regency complex in downtown Minneapolis. Inside I found a résumé and a book proposal sent to me by a magazine editor I respect; in a cover letter she assured me that Suzanne was both a gifted writer and "a person of extraordinary character and superior accomplishment." As a literary agent I had grown accustomed to receiving many such lofty testimonials about potential clients, so I accepted my friend's tribute with more than a grain of salt. And there was another negative factor in play, one that spoke directly to the author's "platform"—what the author brings to the negotiating table that all but guarantees a publisher a handsome profit from publishing the author's work. This was not the way business was conducted when I first entered the book-publishing industry in 1974. But it was most definitely the way business was conducted in 2007. It still is today, which helps to explain why the vast number of titles in the market are self-published.

Although Suzanne had been previously published—a good thing because these days it is a virtual prerequisite in enticing the interest of an agent or publisher—the books she had written were primarily focused on sailing, a passion of hers as it is of mine. Such works, however, hardly speak volumes to a literary agent. Most books on sailing have far too limited a national audience to appeal to a traditional New York–style publisher, the sort my agency solicited.

Nevertheless, I was intrigued, for two reasons that seemed at odds with each other.

According to her curriculum vitae, Suzanne had recently retired from the U.S. Navy after serving our country for twenty years. This indeed intrigued me, because as a teenager I had dreamed of pursuing a similar career path until a football injury in high school and a subsequent 4-F draft classification put an end to such dreams. As I was about to discover, however, had I joined the Navy and become an admiral, I doubt I would ever have been worthy to stand in Suzanne's shadow.

As I continued to read through her résumé, I noted with considerable interest that Suzanne had attained the rank of commander and had served as a commanding officer, arguably the most coveted position a military officer can attain. But there was more—much more—encapsulated on those two pages. During the early years of her career she had earned a master's degree in National Security Affairs, had completed a tour in naval intelligence, and had taught political science at the Naval Academy. A by-the-book officer on her way up through the ranks, she had received one of the highest "top secret" security clearances awarded by our government. She had then served as special assistant to the Chief of Naval Operations and subsequently as aide-de-camp to the chairman of the Joint Chiefs of Staff. She was holding that lofty post when the Twin Towers and the Pentagon were struck during the 9/11 attacks on our country, and was among the first military personnel to witness the damage to those facilities from the air. In the meantime, she had grown both comfortable and influential in the presence of presidents, kings and queens, and other movers and shakers of our global society, whether it was in the bunkers of strategic military command or in offices on Capitol Hill.

*Okay, Commander Giesemann,* I thought as I placed her résumé gently back on my desk, *you have my attention. And my respect.*

As I casually took another sip of coffee, I glanced down at the accompanying book proposal on my desk, expecting to find there the profile of a work either about sailing or about serving in the military. When I noted the title she had given the book, I put down my mug and picked up the five-page proposal.

The proposed title was *The Priest and the Medium,* hardly something one would expect from a retired "no nonsense" naval officer. From the proposal I gleaned the gist of the manuscript: it concerned Anne Gehman—a psychic medium and Spiritualist perhaps best known for her close affiliation with Nancy Reagan—and her marriage to Wayne Knoll, Ph.D., a former Jesuit priest and professor of literature at Georgetown University. So here were two individuals of radically different religious beliefs drawn together by their love for each other and by their love for God. Ms. Gehman is a Spiritualist, one who believes that spirits of the dead reside in a spirit realm and have both the ability and desire to communicate with the living, especially the loved ones they left behind. Her husband, on the other hand, had been trained by the Society of Jesus, a strict religious order of the Catholic Church that repudiates many of the basic principles of Spiritualism, including the probity of mediumship.

Now *this* was interesting. What's more, the proposed book would have no direct competition. The proposal maintained—and my subsequent research confirmed—that Anne Gehman had never before allowed her story to be told. Suzanne had somehow been able to circumvent Ms. Gehman's reluctance to go public with her remarkable story. And the best news? The entire manuscript was finished and ready for immediate review.

I walked the proposal to my partner's office and summarized its contents. He agreed that we needed to request the manuscript, pronto. Which I did, and it arrived by Federal Express the next day. I started reading it that evening and finished it late the next night.

The following morning I called Suzanne at her home in Florida to tell her that my agency would like to represent *The Priest and the Medium*. To my delight she enthusiastically agreed. Apparently our mutual friend, the magazine editor, had had said some nice things about me to Suzanne. So we sealed the deal on the phone, after which Suzanne informed me that she and her husband, Ty, were planning to fly to Minnesota in a couple of weeks. She was a featured speaker at the Minneapolis Boat Show, and would my wife and I like to join her and Ty for dinner after the event?

You bet we would!

It was an enchanted evening, on several levels. The four of us took to each other immediately. That sort of compelling first impression happens rarely in this age of impersonalizing social media, especially when four people are involved; but it happened that evening at Zelo's restaurant on Nicollet Mall in downtown Minneapolis. Conversation flowed easily and comfortably among us, with less attention paid to what was being said and more to the simple pleasure of being in each other's company and enjoying a delicious meal. I did note with interest that Ty—a man of grace, charm, and wit—was also a retired naval officer of considerable renown, the capstone of his brilliant career marked by his promotion to captain of the destroyer USS *John Rodgers*. In sum, it was an evening none of us wanted to see end, but at least it ended with Suzanne's solemn promise to me that our families would remain in close touch as friends in addition to our nascent but promising professional relationship.

Delightful words, and the sort usually said after a memorable social gathering. Little did I know at the time just how deep into my heart and soul Suzanne's promise was soon to go.

⁓

During dinner that evening at Zelo's, we did not share much information about our personal lives. Instead, our back-and-forth focused on publishing and sailing and the brutally cold Minnesota winters—standing in shining contrast to the warmth and glory of Florida winters, as

described in painful (to Victoria and me) detail by both
Ty and Suzanne. In the months that followed, however, I
learned many details of Suzanne's extraordinary transformation from a naval officer orbiting within the stratosphere
of government to an evidential medium. Through representing *The Priest and the Medium* and through numerous
communications with her, I came to learn that two horrific
events—one national in scope and the other intensely personal—had provided the impetus for this transformation.

The first event was the savage airborne attacks on 9/11.
Being at the epicenter of these abominations gave Suzanne
a unique perspective that most Americans, especially those
living far removed from the three areas of impact, simply
did not have. An inquisitive person by nature, as a conse-
quence of these attacks she began an avid pursuit of the
answers to such cosmic questions as, *Why are we here?*
*What happens when we die? Why do so many innocent people
have to die so young? Is this life all there is?* Neither a strong
religious background nor deep-seated religious beliefs
inspired her voracious study. By Suzanne's own admission,
she had no meaningful religious upbringing or training. She
did, however, have moral and hard-working parents who
taught her the difference between right and wrong, and the
inherent rewards of serving humankind.

During these years of thought-provoking study, while
sailing together in the Mediterranean in 2006 following
their retirement from the Navy, Suzanne and Ty received
news from home with the most dreaded words any parent
can hear. Ty's daughter—Suzanne's stepdaughter—Susan,
a twenty-seven-year-old Marine sergeant based at Marine

Corps Air Station Cherry Point, North Carolina, had been struck and killed by a bolt of lightning. Devastated beyond words, Suzanne and Ty flew home from Croatia for the funeral. Afterward, with her husband teetering on the brink of utter despair, Suzanne used the knowledge she had gleaned from her studies to begin meditating, to communicate, if possible, with Susan's spirit. Subsequently, she attended a class on Spiritualism taught by Anne Gehman and went with Ty to consult a medium in search of definitive answers.

Based on the answers she received during that reading, she began writing *The Priest and the Medium*, to show people that mediumship is real and offers the supreme gift of hope and healing. Through Anne Gehman, Suzanne met evidential medium Janet Nohavec. Later, while writing a biography of Ms. Nohavec, Suzanne discovered that she too had the ability to connect with the spirit realm. Encouraged by Ms. Nohavec and others, she decided to study with the best and in 2009 traveled to Stansted, England, to attend Arthur Findlay College, the world's foremost center for the advancement of Spiritualism and psychic sciences.

Upon her return to the United States, Suzanne resolved to use her newly developed skill to communicate with Susan, to assure Ty that his daughter remained steadfastly with him in spirit form; she had not left him and never would. The details of this encounter are best related by Suzanne in her highly acclaimed book *Messages of Hope*, but suffice it to say for the purposes of *this* book that Ty Giesemann—a man who had initially approached mediumship with a doubtful if not disbelieving mind and who recently had commanded military operations from the bridge of a U.S. Navy destroyer— wept openly from the immense comfort of knowing, with absolute certainty, that his beloved Susan was right there in the room with him.

⌒

Not long after Victoria died, I received a call from Suzanne. Her primary concern, of course, was to learn how I was holding up. "I'm getting by, day by day," I told her. "I'm afraid that's the best I can offer."

"I understand, Bill," she said. "Just remember: you don't get over grief. You get through it. And each person is on his or her own timetable. There are no rules and there are no expectations, at least not from anyone who has suffered a grievous loss such as yours. Just know that you are so loved by so many. You are not alone in this."

I thanked her for those kind words and we talked for a few more minutes. When I told her that the memorial service for Victoria would be held four months hence on September 24—the date of our thirty-fourth wedding anniversary—she assured me that she and Ty would fly up from Florida and be there for me and my family.

"Bill," she ventured tentatively before hanging up, "If there is ever anything I can do to help you, you just need to ask."

"You *are* doing something, Suzanne," I said from the heart. "That you and Ty want to come all the way to Minneapolis for the service means everything to me. And to Victoria."

"It's good that you speak of Victoria in the present tense," she said. "I know you know what I mean in saying that."

I knew precisely what she meant. I also knew what she meant by her offer to help. And God knows I wanted to keep an open mind to all possibilities. But my mind in those early days of summer in 2011 was muddled to the extreme. How I managed to get through them remains a mystery, although I give much credit to my sister Cris, many dear friends, and especially my three sons. My sons and I leaned on each other for support, but I will forever maintain that I did the bulk of the leaning. Still, many close friends were concerned about me and my emotional state. On one occasion, while having a cup of coffee with Graham Fenton, my close friend who had served as an Episcopal priest in both South Africa and Minnesota, I was asked if I would ever contemplate suicide.

"No, Graham," I replied without pause. "God would not want me to do that. Victoria would not want me to do that. And I could never do that to our sons."

"I'm glad to hear it," Graham said. "I ask only because I have known a number of people who have done just that at a time like this, and believe me, committing suicide is like dropping an atomic bomb on a family."

I did believe him.

Aside from receiving the kindness and sympathy of friends that summer, I also found comfort in reading and writing, as I always have. During these months, I began a quest similar to Suzanne's after 9/11. I sought answers to the same types of cosmic questions, with heavy emphasis on what happens to the body and soul after death. To my surprise, I found that such topics were no longer considered New Age mumbo-jumbo. They had gone mainstream, and

the books I read (many of which are listed in Appendix A
as recommended reading) were authored by well-known
and highly respected physicians, academicians, theologians,
and even a forensic pathologist. In addition, I read about
people who had experienced firsthand the infinite love of
the spirit realm, either through a near death experience
(NDE) or an out-of-body experience (OBE).

Gradually, day by day, my own resistance to fully embrac-
ing the principles of Spiritualism and mediumship—something I had long been warned about by members of the
clergy and religion teachers—began to crumble. I understood the basis of the Church's opposition to mediumship.
Without question there have been many charlatans and
sharks over the years who have represented themselves as
mediums and who as a result of their fraud have demeaned
the practice of mediumship in the minds of a skeptical
public. And I accepted at that time that there might be
evil spirits out there who were ready, willing, and able to
lead astray a vulnerable soul such as mine, away from the
grace and goodness of God. I got all that. But the one thing
I could not reconcile—after months of deep thought and
study, and after five years of knowing Suzanne Giesemann,
an individual who to my mind personifies the antithesis of
anything bad—was why the Church would seek to deny any
person of any faith the same supreme comfort and joy that
Ty Giesemann had received in the presence of his daughter
in spirit form. Should condoning such manifest expressions
of compassion and love not advance the mission of orga-
nized religion rather than threaten it? Besides, my state of
mind and heart at that time were such that I didn't much

care if evil spirits did exist. If there were just the possibility of communicating with the spirit of my beloved Victoria for but a few minutes, I would seize that chance and gladly walk through the fiery pits of hell for all eternity if that was the price I had to pay.

On a day in mid-July I picked up my telephone and placed a call. It was answered on the second ring.

"Hello? This is Suzanne Giesemann."

"Suzanne, it's Bill."

"Bill!" she exclaimed. "How nice to hear from you. How are you?"

"Getting by," I replied, quickly adding, "Suzanne, I need to ask an enormous favor of you."

"Of course. Ask away."

"Would you do a reading for me?"

"Absolutely," she said without pause, the relief in her voice evident. "Just tell me when."

"Well, my birthday is on the fifth of November. I can't imagine ever receiving a more meaningful birthday gift."

"November fifth it is, then. I'll plan to call you at ten o'clock my time, nine o'clock yours. Does that work for you?"

"Perfectly," I said, swiping at tears welling in my eyes. "Thank you so much, Suzanne."

"Thank you for this opportunity to send you hope," she replied forthrightly. "Now, Bill," she added, "because of this reading, it would be best if Ty and I do not attend the memorial service in September. I know very little about Victoria and your life together, and I don't want to overhear anything at the service that in your mind might compromise the reading. I want a clean slate when we do it. Do you understand?"

"I do, Suzanne," I said. "God bless you."

"God bless you, Bill. God bless us all," she said before we ended the conversation.

As I placed the receiver gently back in its cradle, I felt a warm, blissful sensation settle over me, one I had never before experienced. It was as though I was suddenly being wrapped in a blanket of infinite care and comfort, and lifted up from an abyss of despair and sorrow in the loving hands of a divine source, perhaps one inspired—dear Lord, could it possibly be true?—by Victoria.

Maybe, just maybe, I dared to conjecture, there *was* cause for hope.

*Chapter 6*

*Reading 1*

First, a few definitions and explanations. There is a subtle difference between a **psychic** and a **medium**. A psychic has a supernatural ability to perceive and filter information about people and things on earth that are hidden from the normal senses. (That being said, we all possess some psychic ability. When was the last time you thought of someone and a few minutes later that person called you on the phone?) A psychic does this primarily through a process known as extrasensory perception (ESP). A medium, by contrast, serves as the communication link between physical beings and those who have transitioned to spirit form. While most mediums are also psychics, many psychics are not mediums—at least not in what they practice.

While Suzanne Giesemann is also a psychic, her primary work is as an **evidential medium**, meaning that her mission is to provide conclusive evidence to the **sitter** (in this case, me) that (1) life continues after death, (2) an individual's unique consciousness and personality also continue after death, and (3) the **spirit** present during a reading is in fact the spirit of someone known to the sitter and in most cases dearly beloved by the sitter (in this case, Victoria, who is very dearly beloved). The duty of the sitter is quite simple, however emotional the reading may become: he or she simply confirms or denies the evidence coming through via the medium and says little beyond a simple "yes" or "no" unless encouraged by the medium to say more. The concern is that a lengthy dialogue between sitter and medium during a reading could disrupt the link.

How does a medium deliver such evidence? There is only one way. During a reading, the spirit summoned and prompted by the medium provides information that is known only to the spirit and to the sitter. In other words, the spirit provides information through the medium that the medium could not possibly know and that can be delivered only through a direct connection to the spirit. When such a "match" is realized, it is referred to as a **hit**—or in Suzanne's parlance, a "wow" if it is a particularly significant or meaningful hit.

During the weeks and months leading up to November, Suzanne and I communicated infrequently with each other, and when we did it was strictly to discuss literary matters. She therefore came to the reading with a clean slate insofar as prior knowledge of Victoria and our life together was concerned, exactly as she had intended to do.

As the lingering warmth of late summer blended into the glowing colors of early autumn 2011, I somehow found the strength from a reservoir I hitherto did not know existed in me to deliver a eulogy for my wife at St. Stephen's Church in Edina where several hundred friends and family members had gathered in her honor. I had to do this, even though our priest advised against it because I was still in one of the most difficult periods of the grieving process. As my sons said to me, "Dad, no one else can deliver the emotion at Mom's funeral that you can." They were right, of course. Delivering emotion on that day was not a challenge.

The few weeks between September 24 and November 5 passed as the entire summer had, in a blur. My thoughts were focused on the upcoming reading, of course. I had no preconceived notions of what I would take away from it. I only knew from my study of numerous authorities on the subject of afterlife communications that I would be in communication with a medium (Suzanne) who in turn would be in communication with a presumed spirit (Victoria), and information the medium passed on from the spirit either would or would not resonate with me. I was determined, come what may, to maintain an open mind based on three interlocking convictions: my eternal love for Victoria, my abiding faith in and respect for Suzanne, and the suggestions of spirit presence I had already experienced (profiled in the next chapter). To my mind, the reading could not fail. I was already a believer because my heart told me to be.

On the morning of November 5 I was seated at my desk in my home office at 8:15, even though Suzanne was not due to call me until 9. I knew what she was doing at the moment: meditating, shifting her consciousness up and away from the physical world, setting the intention to connect with the spirit world and asking those spirits who wished to communicate through her to blend their consciousness with hers. Still relatively new to the evolutions of mediumship, she was calling upon her **spirit guides** (collectively known to her as Sanaya) to help ensure that this reading in particular went as well as was humanly and spiritually possible. This was the ultimate gift of love and hope that she yearned to give to me on this special day.

I, too, closed my eyes as I sat at my desk and offered a brief prayer of thanksgiving to God as images of Victoria and memories of our life together floated lovingly through my consciousness. When the telephone rang precisely at nine o'clock I picked up the receiver and wished Suzanne a good morning. After a few brief preliminaries, we started. What follows here in italics (commentary or explanation is in normal type) are excerpts from the actual transcript of what turned out to be a forty-five-minute reading taped in its entirety by Suzanne.

[Sounds of Suzanne inhaling and exhaling]

*Okay. Here we go. Just give me a few seconds, all right?*

*Take all the time you need.*

[Light laughter—Suzanne] *Okay. I will just acknowledge that your father is on the other side. Is that correct?*

*Yes.*

*Yes, and I have made the mistake in the past of blowing off relatives because I want to get to one person in particular. But right away I sense your father. I would not say this unless I felt it, but I sense that you had a very good relationship with him. Is that correct?*

*Yes, it is.*

*And the word I keep hearing is "wise." I don't want him to stick around to get evidence from him, but he is saying that they are taking good care of her. We're taking good care of her.*

*Oh, dear God . . .*

*And he seems like such a gentleman. That's the word that's coming through. You would understand that. He's wearing a suit and looks so dignified. He is a man who would have taken great pride in his appearance. Is that correct?*

Yes, it is.

*Okay. Boy, it's really important to him that you know that she was met and that they are taking good care of her.*

[Choking sound—me] Thank you, Dad.

*Okay. Wow. Thank you for that. Wow. I like order in a reading, Bill, and I like everything in order, but I'm going to give you everything as it flows with no filtering. I'm drawn back now to where I would feel a wife. I have different positions where I feel the energy, which is why I was drawn first to the right side and I knew it was your dad. Now they [Suzanne's spirit guides] are letting me come back to the center and I have a vision of Victoria in a long white diaphanous gown. I don't know why and I don't normally see visions, but there's something about this dress—it's like a wedding dress. And it's floor length and it goes out at the bottom. You would recognize this, she says.*

Yes.

*It is a wedding dress. Why are you showing me that? Why?. . . The most important day of my life, she says. [Sounds of multiple exhales—Suzanne] Okay. Oh. Something about garlands of flowers. Tell me some more [spoken to Victoria]. Welcome, welcome, welcome. She doesn't want to leave this image. Does all this make sense to you so far Bill?*

Yes, it does.

*She doesn't want to leave the wedding vision alone. I believe*

*you had a big and full church wedding because that is clearly
the huge image in my mind. Is that correct?*

Yes.

*Yes. And she was walking down the aisle, she says, and your
eyes met and she was looking at you and it felt as though her
heart was about to burst. It was the happiest day of her life.*
[Choking sounds—me] *Mine, too.*

*Okay. Thank you for that. Okay. Okay. Whew. Some-
thing about travel. I don't know if you two liked to travel or
planned to travel. I'm just hearing the word "travel." And I
got this in the middle of the night and I'm hearing it again. It's
the word "hospice." Was there hospice care at the very end?*

Yes.

*Ah, that's good! I did not know that. Okay. Thank you for
that* [said to Victoria]. *Okay, now give me some more. Okay,
I will tell you the energy I'm feeling now. Very calm, as if nothing could disturb her. It's a sense of peace that is greater than
what most people feel. I don't mean just now. I'm telling you
how she would have been her entire life. Is that correct?*

*Yes, it is.*

*She was a lady, and I mean a lady through and through.
Dignified, poised, and I would stand tall no matter what. If
there was a problem I would hold my head up high and would
instill this [virtue] in my sons as well. Pride and dignity but
without conceit.* [Sounds of labored breathing—Suzanne]
*And love for everybody. This woman loved everybody. It
doesn't feel as though there was a judgmental bone in her
body. Nor an angry bone. She might have flared a bit, but
it would immediately be tamped down. And she would have
been extremely patient and kind. I think Jesus in my mind, and*

*that should be the pattern for everybody, but if anyone could exemplify loving kindness and compassion, it was this woman. Is this accurate?*

Completely.

*So it's not over the top. Because what I feel is . . . oh, she's smiling. Whew. Oh wow. I've got goosebumps now with that one, so that is physical confirmation of spirit presence [sounds of exhaling—Suzanne]. All right. Keep going. Tell me things I could not have known. I saw this in the middle of the night as well: picture frames, everywhere in your house. Beautiful pictures in beautiful frames, all beautifully arranged. Was she into framed pictures?*

Yes.

*She's laughing now, as if this were a private joke between you. You knew that you were not as wonderful as she was, but she thought you were. It's like you looked at her with such admiration because of the person she was, and you would have liked to be as loving and kind as she was. But she's saying, you're right there. Does that make sense?*

Yes, it does.

*Energy level. I have this scale I use. "Zero" is someone who is lethargic and doesn't move around much. And "ten" is someone who is hyper, hyper, hyper, always having to be doing something. She feels . . . hmmm, interesting. She is in the lower half of the scale for her deep sense of calmness. So I would put her at a three just for inner peace. But it moves up the scale to about a six or seven in that she feels a bit industrious. She would be busy and focus on her busyness. She would be purposeful. Does this make sense to you?*

Completely.

*And does the scale resonate with you?*

Completely.

*Good. Okay. All right . . . The two of you. I see you sitting in front of a fireplace reading, as that is much preferred to watching television which she says is for fools.* [Light laughter—Suzanne and me. Victoria often said those very words.]

*Completely agree.*

*Oh. Okay. She's showing me an evening ritual of the drink by the fireplace. I hear the word "ceremony," not just a "ritual." Does this make sense to you?*

Yes.

*Classical music . . . classical music. Did she like classical music?*

Yes.

*Good, because she's showing me a radio tuned to classical music.* [WJIB in Boston—we listened to that station almost every day we lived in Hingham.]

*Wonderful. Keep going. Give me some more. Ah! Hmm. All right. I'm seeing a little porcelain flower. Would you know of something like that around your house? It's a flower about four inches across, and white with maybe a little green in it. Do you recognize that?*

Not right away.

*Okay. That's one of those things that should be written down and you may come across it or remember at some point. Oh, I suddenly see a paintbrush in her hand and she's painting the details of something. Did she ever use a paintbrush?*

Yes, she's an artist.

*Ah! I could not have known that! Yes! Yes! And painting flowers. Did she paint flowers?*

*Yes, she did.* [Among her other paintings of flowers, Victoria's signature work, entitled "Lady at Table," depicts a white flower on the table standing in a porcelain vase roughly four inches across. That image has hung prominently on the wall of our house for many years.]

[Laugh of delight—Suzanne] *Thank you for that. And the detail is important. The detail is important. And she's talking about beauty and she had a deep, abiding love of beauty. There was almost a sacredness about it. She would be one to stop and smell the flowers and appreciate the beauty of them and look at them with an artist's eye. Would she do that?*

*Yes, she would.*

*Okay. Show me some more. Okay, what are you telling me? Oh, she made some elaborate meals and she was a really good, good cook. Is that true?*

*Yes.*

*Yes, and again she's showing me the details. I suspect . . . no, I know she was a perfectionist. Is that correct?*

*Completely.*

*Yes, she's correcting me as I go. Oh, did she love cooking for you and your boys. She loved, loved, loved it. It was not a duty or a chore to her. It was almost like a raison d'être. The skill and care she put into fixing even the most ordinary of meals is how she showed her love for you. Is that correct?*

*Completely.*

[Sounds of exhales—Suzanne] *I'm just hearing from my* [spirit] *guides that I need not have worried about this reading. Okay. Go on. There's something about brown gravy. Brown gravy. Would you understand why she is putting brown gravy on a meal?* [A chuckle of incredulity] *Brown gravy?*

[My own chuckle of incredulity] *I do, actually.*

*Wow. Okay. That one won't go away. So there you go . . .
Okay. All right. Keep going. We got that one. Now tell me
more. Okay. At the risk of bringing up painful memories, there
seems to have been quite a bit of pain at the end. But there's
a sense of stoicism about this. I want to be biting down and
gritting my teeth like I'm not going to complain, I am not going
to complain. Does that make sense to you?*

*Completely.*

*Final minutes. There seems to be more than just you and
your sons in the room with her.*

*No. Just the four of us.*

*It's just that there was more than just the four of you, she
says.*

[Victoria was right, of course. There was also a hospice
nurse present.]

*Oh, book clubs. Was she in a book club?*

*Long ago, yes* [a cookbook club].

*Okay, move on. Again there is such a sense of properness, of
mutual respect. Oh, she's showing you as the guy who is putting his coat out over a puddle, whoever that was* [Sir Walter
Raleigh, for Queen Elizabeth]. *This is obviously a symbol
that you were the perfect gentleman to her.*

*I did that once.*

*You did that?*

*Yes, when we were dating.*

*Oh, my God. So it's not just symbolic.*

*No. I actually did that for her once.* [And ruined my coat
in the process, but who cares? I certainly didn't.]

*Well, that's a "wow." Okay, thank you for that. Whew.*

*Whew. Okay. Oh, God, she loved everything about you, she
says. You could do no wrong in her eyes. Oh boy, the emotion
is so very high. Whew . . . whew. The love is still here, Bill.
That's from her. Those are her words. That can't go away. She's
reaching out and gripping your hand, and your pillow is wet at
night. And you would hold her in your arms at night and stroke
her hair. Such love, such tenderness. This is soul mate love that
so few have. It's what makes it so hard.*

[Choking sounds—me]

*Red roof . . . I have an image of a red roof, but it's symbolic
of where she did not want to go.* [Laughter—Suzanne] *She
had a disdain for cheap motels or hotels. Either we stay some
place in comfort or we don't travel at all. Does that make sense
to you?*

[The image of The Highlands monster came instantly to
mind.] Yes.

*Okay. Let's keep going. Okay. All right. She's showing
me dollar bills. Why am I seeing dollar bills? Why? Hmm . . .
donations. Someone collected money in her honor and gave it
to a charity that she would have appreciated. Is that right?*

Yes [the American Cancer Society].

*There you go. And she is most grateful for that. This is
pretty awesome, huh?*

Utterly awesome. And wonderful.

*Okay, tell me more. Okay. Now there's something about
showers. Tell me about it . . . Oo-oo, warm towels after a
shower. Was there something about you guys and warm
towels?*

Yes, there is. [One memorable Christmas I gave Victoria
a high-end brass towel warmer. She counted it as one of her

favorite gifts ever. She used it every time she took a shower, whatever the season.]

*God, I love it! Beautiful. Okay, give me some more. Let's move on. That fireplace was really special because she keeps taking me back there. Okay, hmm, get it right. You need to light it more, Bill. Is there something about you being afraid to sit in front of the fire because it brings back so many memories?*

Not afraid, but sad.

*Yes, of course. But you're not lighting the fire. First there was an image of you staring at it. But now it's like it has gone cold. Oh, wow. She says, light it and as you stare into the flames you will be able to see her image more clearly and feel her warmth. All right?*

I promise I will do that.

*That becomes a meditative sort of thing, Bill. That's what she's showing me. And do that with peace, and remember the things that came through here as evidence that she is here with you every time you think of her.*

[Exhaling sounds—Suzanne]

[Choking sounds—me]

*That special time: don't be afraid of it because it brings back the sadness. But continue that and you will feel my closeness. Because it's when you think of me that I draw the closest to you. The warmth you feel will be my warmth.*

I understand.

*All right. Okay, my hand goes to a necklace I am wearing. It's not a religious one, but what I am seeing has a crucifix on it, something religious. Did she have such a necklace?*

Not a necklace, but an arm bracelet [made of rosary beads].

*Is Jesus on the cross? It feels like a crucifix, but did it actually have Jesus on it?*

*I don't know. I know there's a cross on it, but she rarely
wore it. It's in her jewelry box. I'll have to take a look. I think
so, actually.*

*Normally I don't see that sort of detail, and it seems important.
So when you find it, please let me know in an email.*

*I will.*

[It took me several days to find Victoria's jewelry box
because my sons had moved everything in the bedroom. It
turned out to be in plain sight on top of the bureau beside
my bed, its presumed obscurity no doubt an indication of
my state of mind at that time. When I opened it, there was
the arm bracelet with a cross on it and Jesus on the cross. I
rushed downstairs to my office to email Suzanne with that
detail. She was delighted to receive it.]

*Bill, I don't know if you recently found some sheets in a
closet. I have this clear image of you holding a bed sheet of hers
to your nose to get her scent. Did this happen?*

[Silence]

*You put your nose in something recently. Did you put your
nose to a sheet to get her scent? Do you understand that?*

*I do, actually* [explanation in next chapter].

*Okay. There's a sense of teaching about her. Did she ever
teach?*

*Yes.* [Her first job after graduating from the Kansas City
Art Institute was as a teacher of art at Penn Valley Community College in Kansas City.]

*Okay. Good. Yay. There's something about her smile that
would melt you.*

*Oh, God, yes.*

*She's pointing at her mouth and smiling radiantly. It lights
up not just her face but the room and certainly you.*

*Yes.*

*It's still there, Bill, she says.*

*Oh, God.*

*Such a lady. I don't think she would have cursed much. Is that correct?*

*Yes. She never swore. Never.*

*Ah, and when your family was together I want to be saying grace. Would you two say grace with your sons?*

*Yes, we would. Every evening. She insisted on it.*

*Okay. Thank you for that. I'm hearing, let me go quietly into the night. I'll let you interpret that.*

*I can.*

*And I'm told it has a dual meaning. It also means she was peaceful when she slipped away. Is that correct?*

*Yes.*

*Okay. She's showing me this very clearly. Her arms go up and she is surrounded by light. Surrounded by light. It's a sense of peace far beyond the sense of peace that pervaded her here [on the physical plane]. I've never gotten this in this way before. She is at such peace. Usually I get, "Oh, I'm so happy," or "Oh, I feel so much love." This is an all-pervading peace. And I was about to say, a peace like you couldn't imagine. But I'm corrected. It was a peace she did imagine. Do you understand that?*

*Yes.*

*It's as if she had a sense of what awaited her, and the reality is how she envisioned it. She's completely at peace and she wants you to be, too. You are just beginning to find that. Don't rush it, she says, and this [reading] will help.*

*Yes.*

*Okay . . . What is that? Hmm. Her left arm is suspended up. Why? Lifting you up? I don't know.* [Spoken to Victoria:] *What were you getting at a minute ago? Okay. Normally I see or feel a kiss or a hug, but instead, Victoria is turning around and backing up against you and feeling your arms going around her waist, with her back against your chest and your head going next to hers. It's a total embrace that way. Do you get this image?*

[I did, so much so I was unable to speak for several moments. Especially during our early years in Virginia and Massachusetts, but continuing on occasion in Minnesota, I would sneak up behind Victoria while she was working in the kitchen and wrap my arms around her waist. She would always protest—which was part of the fun because she always enjoyed it—and we would sway back and forth in the position described above, in an intimate embrace that was, as far as we knew, unique to us.]

*Do you get this image, Bill?*

*Yes.*

*Good. So that's about it. Do you have any questions, Bill?*

[Multiple choking sounds—me] *No questions. But if you could tell her something for me . . .*

*I don't have to tell her. There's no distance here. She knows your every thought. She's just talking to you through me. So think what you want to say in your mind, or say it out loud.*

*I'll say it out loud: Dearheart, I love you with all my heart and I will for eternity.* [More choking sounds] *That's what I want her to know.*

*Oh, God. And she says, how could there be any doubt? You didn't need to say anything. That goes without saying. But she hears it and she knows it. Just know that love is still here and it will never die. She draws me to the image of your father meeting her at the beginning of this reading, to say that she will be the first person to meet you on the other side. No matter what happens in your life, no matter who you meet, it doesn't matter. She will be the first person you meet. Nothing could ever match the love that you two share.*

[Choking sounds—me] *And please tell her that I will never, never take off my wedding ring. Not ever.*

*Something about someone having to cut your finger off to get it off. She just said that to me. Does that make sense to you?*

Yes. It did.

## Chapter 7

## *Spirit Presence*

Just as what happened on May 1, 2011, changed my life in one way, what happened on November 5 changed my life in quite a different way. On May 1 my beloved bride of thirty-four years died, and despite my strict religious upbringing I feared I had lost her forever. Then, six months later, I got her back, forever. The comfort and healing that comes with *knowing* I will see her again cannot be expressed in words. Such a blissful sense of peace, love, and joy spills from the heart, not the pen.

I realize that not all readings go as well as mine with Suzanne did. A host of challenging issues can confront a medium, including a weak link to the spirit world or the sudden appearance of an unexpected visitor seeking redress for perceived misdeeds committed when that spirit was in physical form. And I realize there are skeptics out there who will claim that three of four "hits" during a reading are the result of the medium either reading the mind of the sitter or having foreknowledge of the sitter as the result of prior research. But skeptics take heed: during my forty-five-minute reading I counted (after listening to the recording multiple times) fifty-four distinct hits. Nor did I count as a hit any piece of evidence that was generic in nature. For example, to the question, "Did you and Victoria call each other 'darling' at times?" the answer is yes, we did, but so do countless other couples. So I didn't count that "match" as a hit. As to a psychic reading my mind, I believe the evidence of the rosary bracelet with a crucifix attached to it discounts that possibility, since I was not able to confirm that piece of evidence until several days after the reading. Equally to the point, not one piece of evidence presented during the reading made no sense to me. Each piece represented a hit of one degree or another.

Each of the fifty-four hits registered in that first reading was a piece of evidence known only to my immediate family—and in many cases, only to Victoria and me. There is, however, one notable exception to that last statement.

When Suzanne, prompted by Victoria, asked me, "Bill, I have this clear image of you holding a bed sheet of hers to your nose to get her scent," I froze, not able to immediately respond. During the last days of her illness while she was still living at home, Victoria became incontinent. On one occasion she stripped the sheets off the bed and crumpled them up in the corner of her closet to hide the evidence from me. A few days after her death, while going through her belongings in her closet, I came across that sheet and held it to my nose to decide whether to wash it or discard it.

While I realize that this sort of description is hardly appropriate for dinnertime conversation, the ramifications of it most definitely are, for it raises two critical issues. The first issue is that only one physical being knew that I had gone into her closet to retrieve a bed sheet, and that person is me. Until now, I have not shared this experience with anyone, including my sons. Why would I? And yet, *someone* witnessed me doing that. As to who that someone was, I think we can all agree that the list of potential candidates is quite short.

The second important issue is that as much as I wanted to converse with Victoria in spirit form, Victoria wanted to converse with me in physical form. The lines of communication between the physical and spirit realms go both ways, as does the desire to communicate and to provide comfort and healing to a loved one. The piece of evidence inherent in the soiled bed sheet is undoubtedly one of the most dramatic ways Victoria could imagine to convince me that she lives on in spirit form and remains with me and our sons 24/7.

As an aside, the first reading did not end where the previous chapter ends. It continued for another five minutes or so, the messages of love in those final minutes devoted to her three sons, each of whom she loves dearly.

⌒

Earlier that year, shortly after Victoria's death, I received my first awareness of possible spirit presence. I use the word "possible" because there is no way I can prove anything. I know what I believe, but I do not represent what follows here and in chapter 9 as "proof" of spirit presence, as I do the evidence embedded in the three separate readings Suzanne conducted.

During the three weeks that Victoria was in Methodist

Hospital in Minneapolis, we received three visits from our Episcopal priest, a lovely and very spiritual woman who each time brought great consolation and empathy to both Victoria and me. The three of us talked, reminisced, and prayed together; on at least one occasion we even shared some light laughter. On her third and last visit, after Victoria had been admitted to hospice and had drifted off to sleep, Nancy invited me to have a cup of coffee with her in the hospital cafeteria.

"Bill," she said at one point, "soon after Victoria passes, she may try to communicate with you. It doesn't always happen, but if it does, it can come in a variety of ways. The most common way is through an animal or a bird."

Although I had not yet started my extensive research into afterlife communications, I had heard of this phenomenon. Recently I had read an account of the sudden death of a man who for years had studied the habits and habitats of bald eagles. He was fascinated by these magnificent birds and wanted to know everything he could about them. Shortly after his death, his devastated wife was wandering aimlessly in their backyard when a bald eagle swooped down just above her head, lit on a tree branch at the far end of the yard, and then swooped over her again. These evolutions were repeated several times, and each time the eagle lit on a branch, it remained there for a time staring at the woman below in the yard. This behavior amazed the woman, but what made it even more stupefying to her was that she had never before seen a bald eagle in the wild. Her home was in the Bluegrass region of Kentucky, far removed from water, forests, and other habitats favored by these birds. Still, after reading the account, I had a hard time accepting that the spirit of the woman's husband had somehow blended his consciousness with the consciousness of the eagle to get it to do something that merited his wife's rapt attention. It was simply counterintuitive.

"Does Victoria have a favorite animal or bird?" Nancy asked me.

"She loves all of God's creatures," I replied. "But her favorites, hands down, are rabbits and deer. We have both in abundance in our backyard—for a good reason. Each day, Victoria cuts up carrots and scatters the pieces on the lawn near where the rabbits have a nest. She also puts out apples for the many deer that parade across our lawn—much to the consternation of our neighbors, I might add. Those deer eat their shrubs and greenery as much as they do ours. But Victoria doesn't care. She loves to gaze out the kitchen window and watch as the animals enjoy the food she left for them."

"Well then," Nancy said, smiling, "I urge you to keep your eyes and mind open to the possibilities."

"I promise I will," I said.

Three days after Victoria died, I arose with the first tinge of dawn, unable to sleep, again. After splashing some cold water on my face, I ambled downstairs to the kitchen, made some coffee, and then took a cup with me into the living room, where I flicked on the gas fireplace and sat down next to the sofa on which Victoria had sat nearly every evening during the fourteen years we had lived in that house. Sadness required only a few minutes to overcome me, and when it did, I wandered back to the kitchen, ostensibly to reheat my coffee in the microwave. As the machine hummed to life and thirty seconds began ticking away, I turned around, walked to the picture window, and gazed out at our expansive back lawn. It was the exact spot at which Victoria had stood so often, watching animals foraging for food or our sons playing their ball game du jour.

To my surprise I saw, not twenty feet away, two rabbits sitting on their haunches staring back at me as though they were in some sort of trancelike state. What truly surprised me, however, was that I had never seen rabbits like these before. They were not the gray-furred little critters that had so eagerly nibbled away at the carrot smorgasbords that Victoria had laid out each day for them. These two rabbits were blonde-haired and sported floppier ears. And they were considerably larger than those other fellows. In fact, they looked more like hares than rabbits.

We had stared at each other through the window for some time when suddenly the two animals jumped toward me, cutting the distance between us in half. Then, to my utter stupefaction, they reared up on their substantial hind legs, paused for a moment, and then, in almost perfect synchrony, leapt up high into the air, not once, not twice, but three times before alighting to earth, where they again hunched down and stared at me.

By this time the intermittent beeping of the microwave reminded me that I needed to remove my mug from inside. When I turned around to do that, and then turned back, the rabbits were gone. I walked out to the backyard in search of any trace of them, to no avail. I never saw either of those rabbits again.

A question nags at me. If Victoria's spirit was in control

of one of those rabbits—as I devoutly believe it was—whose spirit was in control of the other one? There are a number of possibilities, but the most likely is either my sister Diana, who had also passed on from cancer several years earlier, or my cousin Daphne, who was a close friend of Victoria and had suffered from cerebral palsy her entire life on earth.

⌒

I have also come to believe that souls in the spirit realm can act as spirit guides to their loved ones left behind in the physical world. They are not just "here." They can actually be proactive in helping their loved one when the loved one needs their help.

My fist indication of this phenomenon occurred two years after Victoria's death as I was struggling to reinvent myself as an editor and ghostwriter. My third novel had recently been published to critical acclaim, and those endorsements lent credibility to my cyberspace "open for business" sign. Still, I was encountering the same sorts of challenges that all entrepreneurs face, whether their business plan profiles a "one man band" such as mine or a more substantial venture.

Soon after I moved from our home in Minneapolis to the nearby lakeside town of Wayzata, a business opportunity arose that appealed to me for two reasons. First, it involved a historical novel, the same genre as my own novels. And second, the fee would be substantial because it involved developmental editing, a form of editing that demands more skill and time—and thus merits higher fees—than more straightforward copy editing. The author was an attorney working out of a private office in Minne-apolis who had contacted me after hearing about me from another client of mine. After several meetings with the lawyer during which he seemed more than receptive to the proposed assignment, I sent him, at his request, a letter of agreement that detailed how the professional relationship would unfold during a projected six-month period, the key elements of which we had already discussed.

What happened next was truly remarkable. On a Thurs-day in early May I received an email from the author, thanking me for sending him the letter but also informing me that, regretfully, he would not be able to act on it. He had two children in college, he reminded me, and after long and prayerful deliberation he had decided that making a substantial investment in the editing of his novel was not in the cards, at least not at the moment. He concluded with the words that no entrepreneur likes to hear, that he would be happy to revisit the situation at some point in the more distant future when his own cash flow was more accommodating.

I thanked him for his kind consideration, of course, and I wished him well. I then pulled up an Excel spreadsheet with my annual budget. With a heavy heart, I deleted the anticipated monthly inflows that would have resulted from an assignment I had incorrectly assumed was "a done deal."

The next morning, as my oldest son and I were pre-paring to run out for a few groceries, I walked down to the lobby of our apartment complex to get our mail. As I sorted through the envelopes while we were on the way to Target, I came across one from Social Security. Inside was the dire-sounding message that because I had earned "too much money" during the previous tax year (I had not yet reached the age of sixty-six, when such limitations on allowable earned income no longer apply), I was being penalized by having my monthly benefit denied for seven months, the period of time necessary to repay Social Security for my perceived excesses. Worse, the withholding of funds was to begin immediately, meaning that I would not be receiving the May payment due the following Wednesday. If the matter had not been so serious I would have had a good laugh over what one of our government agencies deems "too much money" being earned by one of its beneficiaries. But to be fair, I knew beforehand what those limitations were.

To me, what had just happened was the definition of a "double whammy." Not only did I not land the editing contract with the lawyer, I was being cut off from my Social Security benefits for the balance of the year. And reparations were to begin in a few days, before I could possibly generate new business from other potential clients. Working on my Excel budget that evening, I realized, was not going to be a pleasant experience.

"What do I do *now*, Dearheart?" I remember asking out loud as my son drove us back to the apartment. It was a rhetorical question. I certainly was not expecting an answer. I was simply felling hemmed in and overwhelmed, again missing Victoria's calm and reassuring ways with every fiber of my being.

After my son and I returned home and put away the groceries, I went into my home office to check emails. To my surprise I saw on the list of unread mail a message from the lawyer author. I clicked on it and then read some of the most welcomed words I have ever received in business.

"Bill," the email stated, "I've had a change of heart. Don't ask me why. I can't explain it. But I have signed the Agreement Letter and enclosed the first check. You should receive them on Monday, Tuesday at the latest. I look forward very much to working with you."

If this had been a one-time event, I might agree with those skeptics who insist that the sequence of events described above is nothing more than a series of extraordinary coincidences. But it didn't happen just once. It has happened multiple times. Simply stated, when I needed help the most during those formative and difficult years, help arrived. The Bible says, "God will provide," and without question God has shone His favor on me and my family in the most merciful of ways. And I will forever believe that one of my own spirit guides—my own beloved Victoria—has played an active and critical role in my deliverance.

*Someone* had to have planted the seed in the lawyer's brain to change his mind so quickly and radically.

⌒

During the previous fall, in 2012, two people near and dear to my heart suffered a grievous loss similar to my own. In late October I received a package from Pat Brodecky Leavell, Victoria's closest friend when she was growing up in Howells. Inside was a letter informing me that her husband, John, had suffered a heart attack and had died in her arms. Also enclosed were an Order of Service for John's funeral and several photographs of Pat and Victoria playing together as little girls.

Pat had been one of Victoria's bridesmaids in 1977, but since then our communication with her and John had been mostly via Christmas cards and an occasional letter. Family pressures, especially after we began raising our own family, prevented us from getting together; that and the fact that we lived far apart. Nevertheless, I knew from countless conversations with Victoria how close she and "Birdie" had been in their youth and how close they remained. They called themselves "blood sisters for life."

I immediately placed a call to Pat and we talked for a lengthy period. Minutes into the conversation she broke down in tears and was inconsolable—then and during a number of subsequent phone calls. She was utterly bereft, for reasons I well understood. At a time like that, for someone in my position, the best thing to do is to be still and listen. I understood from my own experience that being able to talk about your deceased loved one to someone who clearly is both sympathetic and empathetic can be thera-peutic, at least in the short term.

And yet I so wanted to do something material to help Pat beyond just listening and being a friend. So I sent her a recording of my first reading with Suzanne—something I had done only for my sister Cris and for Graham Fenton, the Episcopal priest I mentioned in chapter 5—in the devout hope that she would recognize enough of Victoria in the reading to know that Victoria was still with me, and with her. And if Victoria was still with her, so was John.

In sum, she was overwhelmed by the reading, but Pat

being Pat, she was hesitant to ask the obvious question of me. She is simply not one to ask for favors or special consideration. So it was up to me to ask it for her. "Pat," I said during one of our phone calls, "I have taken the liberty of talking to Suzanne on your behalf. She wants to help you. If you're willing, I urge you to give her a call."

Pat promised me she would. And she did.

Two months later, early in the morning on the day after Christmas, I received a tearful call from Cris, who told me that her beloved husband, Tom, had died in her arms during the night. Tom had been in poor health for some time, so his passing was not unexpected—although the finality of death is *always* devastating to loved ones, no matter what the mitigating circumstances.

Although Cris is a strong and pragmatic woman, she too had a difficult time navigating the many shoals and reefs that inevitably manifest themselves during a period of intense grief. She is my sister, so obviously I wanted to console her. In addition, no one except my sons had "been there for me" more than Cris during my own heart-wrenching early stages of grief.

She was the first to broach the subject of Suzanne, since she had listened to the recording of my first reading. I of course assured her that I would speak to Suzanne—I had been contemplating doing just that since the day after Christmas—although I cautioned her to let some weeks and even months pass before having a reading of her own. If a reading is conducted too soon after a passing, the emotion of being reunited with a loved one, regardless of how desperately that reunion might be desired, can be so awe-inspiring and overwhelming that it can reduce the sitter to a state resembling shock, My own first reading took place six months after Victoria passed on, and it left me with those very same emotions. That day and for days afterward I wandered about aimlessly as the blissful reality of what had occurred during my reading—and what that reality *meant*— began to register deep within my heart and soul.

Cris agreed. She called Suzanne, and they arranged for a reading a few weeks hence. It was yet another gift bestowed on my family by Suzanne, because by this time she was doing all the readings she could emotionally handle, and the waiting list of people requesting an audience with her—as a medium and/or as a speaker—was growing by leaps and bounds.

Both readings went well, as I was quite certain they would. Within an hour after her reading Cris called me on the phone.

"Suzanne nailed it," were her first words. "Her first image was of Tom with a fiddle"—Tom's favorite of the many musical instruments he played—"and it all went uphill from there. She really nailed it!"

"No, Cris," I said softly, "Suzanne didn't nail it. You and Tom did."

In due course Cris sent me a copy of her reading, just as I had sent her one of mine. On the evening I received it, I poured a glass of Bordeaux and played the recording on my computer. It was an unforgettable hour. No doubt about it: that was the spirit of Tom Endicott, my brother-in-law, actually sharing a dialogue with my sister, his wife, through the enabling grace and kindness of Suzanne Giesemann. After the recording was over, I poured a second glass of wine and lifted it in a toast to Cris and Tom—and of course to Victoria.

Pat's reading was also a success, insofar as it confirmed John's presence in spirit form. But her reaction to the reading was different than Cris's. It may have imbued Pat with hope and faith, but it also made her miss John's physical presence all the more. Knowing he was with her in spirit form made her yearn to put her arms around him and hug him as she had so lovingly done so many times over so many years. And as more days elapsed, the immediacy of the reading began to fade. Gradually the dogmatic "let's get real" side of her brain kicked in and she found herself questioning the reading and returning to her former level of grief, despondent over her "failure" to "feel" John's presence in her daily life the way I felt and continue to feel Victoria's presence. My saying to her that perhaps her mind was too muddled and cluttered to be receptive to signs that John might be trying to send her appealed to her on an intellectual level but not as much on an emotional level. She withdrew into herself and sought consolation by driving to Montana and other destinations where she and John had gone camping together, hoping to somehow commune with her husband in the places they had shared and loved in their married life. Above all, she sought further "proof" that John was indeed with her and would never leave her.

I understood Pat's emotions—I had suffered through many of them myself—but still I was worried about her. When I expressed my concerns to Suzanne while she was on a book and speaking tour across the United States and Canada, she offered an unusual solution.

"As you know, Bill," she said, "Ty and I are planning to spend a few days in Minneapolis on our way back to Florida. We'll be there in mid-September. You had mentioned that Cris might fly up from Arizona at that time. Will she, do you think?"

"Absolutely," I assured her. "There's no way she'd miss this opportunity to meet you in person. And to thank you for giving her husband back."

"Wonderful. I look forward to meeting her as well. Now, do you think Pat would be willing to come up from Nebraska at that same time?"

"I don't know. I can ask her. Why?"

"Well, Ty and I would like to throw a party for you one evening right here in our coach."

"A party? You mean for Cris, Pat, and me?"

"Yes. And we would also like to invite Victoria, Tom, and John."

It took a moment for her words to sink in. "Do you mean you would host a three-way reading?"

"Sure. Why not? It may not be the norm, but I have every confidence we can do it. And if not, we'll have plenty of wine and hors d'oeuvres on hand to enjoy afterward."

I immediately called Cris to tell her about Suzanne's invitation. She was thrilled, as I knew she would be. I then called Pat, who was out for the evening. So I sent her an email that summed up the details of a proposed "party" that would take place several weeks hence.

The next morning I received a reply from Pat that warmed my heart.

"My bag is packed," she wrote.

*Chapter 8*

*Reading 2*

Ty and Suzanne had a good reason to stop over in Minneapolis for several days on their way home to Florida. Aside
from visiting friends in the area, Suzanne was scheduled to
speak on Sunday afternoon at the Lake Harriet Spiritual
Center in an area of Minneapolis known as Uptown.

Since I had already attended several of Suzanne's presen-
tations, I knew from firsthand experience how she is able
to enthrall her audiences: she exudes an irresistible combi-
nation of compassion and reason blended with a heartfelt
enthusiasm for her mission of helping people find comfort
from knowing that their loved ones never leave them, and
that love never dies. As in every previous presentation I
had attended, at its conclusion the audience rose as one to
give her a sustained standing ovation.

On the previous day, Cris, Pat, and I had passed time
along the shores of Lake Minnetonka discussing the "party"
that was to take place a few hours hence. We also talked
about the mischief that Pat and Victoria ("Vicki" to Pat and
others who knew her in her youth) often got into growing up in Howells. I always look for ways to prompt such

conversations because I crave details about my wife's life before I met her.

At six o'clock we drove in Pat's car out to the suburban campsite where Ty and Suzanne had parked their coach. Not every site can accommodate such a vehicle. When I was given my first tour through its substantial interior I thought the Giesemann coach seemed like the highway version of Air Force One. But I had to bear in mind that since Ty and Suzanne live in this coach for much of the year—carrying their messages of hope from state to state and province to province—it serves as a second home to them, the equivalent of the cabin "up north" owned by many thousands of Twin Cities residents.

When we arrived at the campsite at 6:45 Ty met us outside the coach and told us that Suzanne was still meditating and asked if we would mind waiting with him for a few minutes.

"Given what we're waiting for, Ty," I said, "we wouldn't mind waiting out here for a few hours." Cris and Pat readily agreed.

At seven o'clock the side door to the coach opened and Suzanne invited us inside. She, of course, had long since configured the seating arrangements. I was seated in a comfortable chair at one front-end of the "living room," Cris was seated to my left on a sofa, and Pat was seated next to her and across from Suzanne. Ty, meanwhile, had settled into the substantial driver's seat and had swiveled it around to face inward. This was to be his first time attending one of Suzanne's readings, and his role that evening was to both transcribe and record what was being said, and to serve as sommelier and put out the hors d'oeuvres when the reading was over. Although these may not have been his customary duties while holding court in the captain's cabin on board the USS *John Rodgers*, Ty seemed quite content with his assignments.

As a point of interest, this was my first reading with Suzanne in person, and the first time I was able to watch her as the reading progressed. Throughout most of the reading she kept her eyes closed in order to, as she later put it, "shut out most distractions and focus fully on what I am seeing, hearing, or feeling through the connection." At times she would squint and cock her head as she absorbed the verbal and visual communications emanating from the spirit realm. Sometimes she would move her hands about to illustrate what she was seeing before actually saying what she was seeing; at other times she would smile and throw her head back in delight at what a spirit was telling her. The only time she looked directly at me (or at Cris or Pat) was to verify or question a piece of evidence that had come through. She would then return her full attention to the spirit.

Suzanne opened the reading by asking us to hold hands while she offered a prayer of gratitude to God for the love we in physical form shared with each other and continue to share with our loved ones in spirit form. Then, after a few preliminaries, we started in.

Suzanne: *I'm nervous, there's all this energy in here, so it will take a while to go and then it will just take off.*

We three: *There's no hurry.*

*. . . Somebody here had a heart attack. My heart just palpitated.*

Pat: *John did.*

*And someone was a teacher.*

Cris: *Tom was a teacher.*

*Tom was a teacher. I don't think I knew that. Maybe I did. Great . . . and I sense someone had pains in the head.*

Bill: *That could be Tom.*

Cris: *Yes, it's Tom. He had pain everywhere* [in his later years].

*And a feeling of pills. Someone took many pills.*

Pat: *That's John.*

*Okay. Wow, there's been a total shift of energy. I think that Victoria has stepped in. Something about fingernails. Did she take good care of her fingernails?*

Bill: *Yes, she did.* [I often teased her about it until she signed me up for a manicure. I then let the matter drop.]

*Well, she would be ashamed of mine* [light laughter]. *She just said, "I am so at peace," and she's aware of you adjusting a little better.*

*Yes. A little.*

*I see a model sailboat. A toy sailboat. The kind you would sail on a pond. Did you have a sailboat that floated and you could sail it?*

*We did, actually. She gave me one years ago.*

*Yes, she's showing me that. Keep going. Okay, now I want to be flying a kite. Did you two like to fly kites?*

*Yes.*

*It's as clear as day. Now she's talking about dreams of flying and feeling so free.*

*I think I know what that means.*

[Laughter—Suzanne] *She's talking about hair on her arms.*

Pat: *That's from her childhood.*

I just love when this happens. Good. Tell us about it.

*We used to laugh about it. We were both . . .* [Pause]

Go ahead.

*I don't know, we were just kids and we'd say, "Oh my God, look at how hairy our arms are!" We thought we were freaks.*

Excellent. You see why I'm laughing. Spirits bring up the craziest things Hairy arms? It's why I knew it would be wonderful having synergy with other people here. I'm not going to worry about giving equal time to everyone. It's their show and that's how it is. One person will fade out and another person will come back in. Right now Victoria is talking and she is saying that just like you [meaning Suzanne], if there's a sliding board, I'll go down it. Is that right?

Bill: *She loved slides.*

Pat: *Yes. She loved slides as a child.*

Bill: *And as an adult.*

What I love is that she told me this because she knows what I like . . . There's an overwhelming flood of love coming at you, Bill.

[Choking sound—me] And coming right back to her.

I'm hearing the song "I could have danced all night. I could have danced all night, and still have asked for more."

*She used to sing that song when we danced together.* [I always wanted to join in, but I never wanted the poor quality of my singing voice to ruin the moment.]

I could cry the emotion is so high. Such great memories. [Sounds of exhaling—Suzanne] Something about her hair. As though splitting hairs. Very fine hair. Does this make sense?

*She had very fine* [i.e., thin strands of] *hair at the end.*

*Did some of it come out?*

*Yes.*

*Okay, go back to some of those great memories.* [Looking now at Pat] *She doesn't seem like the sort of girl to skip out of school, but you did some naughty stuff together.*

[General laughter]

Bill: *We were just talking about this very subject a couple of hours ago.*

Suzanne, to Pat: *You guys would run off and do stuff that would get most kids in trouble.*

Pat: *We climbed up to the ballroom roof during PE one time, and another time we slid down the fire escape to the school. Silly things like that.*

Suzanne: *And this tells you two things: she is not only with you now, she was with you when you were talking about this. And she took me right over to you* [Pat] *as she said that. And there's a message to you, Cris. Something about the "sacred mother." I don't know what that means. Something about religion and being supportive.*

Bill: *Cris has been very supportive* [to me and the boys].

*Yes, at the time, but she's referencing now something about religion.*

Bill: *Cris, we were just saying that you were not terribly religious growing up, but now you are.*

Cris: *I am. Maybe she's acknowledging my spirituality.*

[Although this was not brought up during the reading, upon reflection I believe that Victoria was referring primarily to the sacred role that Cris stepped into as the boys' surrogate mother following Victoria's death. It has meant everything to them. And to me. And to Victoria.]

*Yes . . . All right. She's showing me little pieces of fabric. Little squares. A collage? Montage? It doesn't feel like a quilt. Collage? Or perhaps a jacket made of many different bright colors. Does that make sense to you?*

Bill: *Actually, it does. I can explain that later. Or now, if you'd like.*

*Sure.*

*Well, there was a* [clothing] *salesman in* [Delray Beach,] Florida [where in earlier years my family used to spend every spring break] at A. *George & Sons who tried for years to get* [my father] *to buy me this incredible Madras coat comprised of many squares of different colors.* I hadn't been in Delray Beach for twenty years when Victoria and I walked into that store and the very same salesman came up and tried to sell me that very same sort of coat, twenty years later. Honest, I'm not making this up. Victoria almost collapsed, she was laughing so hard. [And we talked about it for years afterward.]

*Such a perfect memory to bring up. I have the sense she was not the greatest seamstress. Is that true?*

*That's true. She wasn't.*

*Did you just see me do this?* [Suzanne jerking her hand up] *She just stuck me with a needle as if she would have done it to herself.*

[Laughter]

*And she would have.*

*But, she says, I could cook up a storm.*

*Yes, that she could do.*

*Yes, and she said it word for word. Candles . . . candles . . . I see candles everywhere.*

*Victoria collected candles. We had them all over the house.*

Cris: *That could also apply to Tom.*

*Yes. But I'm still with Victoria. We'll stay with her for a little while longer.*

Bill: *I'm not complaining.*

[Light laughter]

*She's showing me a chain-link fence that you wouldn't know about. And what looks like railroad tracks.* [To Pat:] *Did you say you climbed a chain-link fence? Was it around the school?*

Pat: *It could be the time we tee-peed the new post office.* [General laughter] *After religion class.*

Bill: *Perfect timing, Pat.*

[More laughter]

Suzanne, to Bill: *She's pointing at her neck as if to say either you or she had a neck injury or injuries. Did you?*

*Yes. In my forties I had serious spinal problems, especially in my neck.*

*Yes . . .* [Gentle laughter—Suzanne] *Sometimes I don't want to say things that I hear.*

Pat: *Say it!*

Suzanne, to me: *It's a problem with a zipper. She's laughing about it. Did you have a problem with a zipper?*

*I'm not sure I should answer that.*

[General laughter]

*Well, it's what she's showing me and she's laughing about it. I think she's being a little impish here.*

[Louder laughter]

*She's showing me a bracelet and it's made of gold. And it's engraved.*

*I once gave her an engraved gold bracelet as a gift* [an anniversary gift from Boston jeweler Shreve, Crump & Low, engraved with the date September 24, 1977]. *She always said it was one of her favorite gifts.*

Nice.

*Very nice.*

*She says you always had the best taste. It was as though you were inside her mind and knew what she wanted.* [Light laughter—Suzanne]. *And she says she didn't do too badly herself.*

No.

*Let's move on . . .* [Sound of exhaling—Suzanne] *Something about firecrackers. Did you have a lot of firecrackers in your house?*

*We had a lot of firecrackers. Compliments of her three sons.* [Light laughter]

*Hmm . . . She says you never stopped taking notes on notebook paper. Notebook paper.*

Yes. All the time [usually in reference to my writing].

*And you never stopped thinking. It was as though she could see you thinking even while you slept at night.*

*She used to tell me that.*

*And she had a thing about crawling bugs. Ants. More than most people. Something about "I can't stand it."*

Yes. *Any insect on the kitchen floor was not something she enjoyed.*

*Yes, but what woman does enjoy that? No, it's more than that. It's like, this is totally unacceptable.*

Pat: *She freaked out at camp.* [Laughter] *There was a big spider in our cabin and she was up on her bunk, screaming.*

*Okay, that is definitely not the norm!* [Laughter] *That camp . . . I'm seeing you two in a canoe splashing each other with water.*

Pat: *We almost went over a waterfall. She and I were together with a camp counselor in the canoe. We were paddling toward it* [the waterfall] *and the counselor was screaming at us, trying to get us to turn around. We couldn't seem to turn the canoe around and we splashed each other and we thought it was hysterically funny at the time.*

[Laughter]

*And she's showing me a horrible striped gray mattress and it looks as if you two wrote names on it.*

Pat, in a high-pitched squeal: *We may have done that. Oh, my God. Oh, my goodness.*

Suzanne: *Did you do that?*

*Yes. We did exactly that.*

Bill: *That's a wow.*

Pat: *Camp Kiwanis . . . holy moly . . . hi, Vicki.*

[Light laughter]

*Okay, thank you . . . Yeah, you two were worried about hair on your arms, but who was the one worried about hair on the upper lip?*

Pat, in the same high-pitched tone: *Oh, my God.*

Bill: *I think we just got your answer.*

[Laughter]

Pat: *Yup. Yup. Oh, my God!*

*What got me the most is how insistent she was. "Say it to her, say it to her," she kept insisting.*

Bill: *This is just wonderful.*

*Okay, I think this still has to do with you two* [meaning Pat and Victoria]. *A penchant for chocolate cake and chocolate frosting.*

Pat: *Okay. One of us was having a problem with a boy and*

her dad owned a grocery store. *So she had a key—or she stole
her dad's key—and we broke into the store and we took one of
those Sara Lee cakes and we went down to the tennis courts
and ate the whole thing.*

Bill: *I'm learning a lot about my wife.* [General laughter]
*And I'm learning a lot about Pat, too.* [More laughter]

Pat: *We were good together. We were good together.*

Suzanne: *Okay. Thank you for that. Tonight, have a glass
of wine for her. "Have one for me," she says.*

⌒

At this point in the reading Victoria steps aside and Tom
comes in. The dialogue between him and Cris becomes
emotionally charged. He thanks her for her tenderness and
care especially during his later years when Cris, he says,
pulled him up from the abyss. He called her his cheerleader
and reminded Cris that one of his favorite foods was falafel.
[I had never heard of falafel until that moment and had no
idea what it was.] But Tom being Tom, he could not resist
ending his dialogue with a piece of wit. He tells Cris that
he is at peace, he is flying free, he loves her very much, and,
perhaps most tellingly, he has made amends with another
spirit who means a great deal to him but with whom he had
issues in human form. *See?* he tells Cris. *You can teach an
old dog new tricks!*

Pat's husband, John, then assumes center stage, and
his back and forth with his wife also becomes emotionally
charged. The love they continue to share is obvious from the
evidence and words exchanged between them. He tells her
that he is very much aware of the love letters to heaven that

Pat continues to write to him. *Keep writing; I read every word,* he assures her. *You have no idea how much we* [meaning those in spirit form] *hear your thoughts and are in your thoughts, and writing amplifies it because your thoughts are more focused and you are holding his energy.* But John has a concern. He knows that Pat remains steeped in grief and feels alone, and he wants to help her heal. He urges her to make more of an effort to get out and volunteer for some cause and meet people. And he gently shakes her shoulders and says: *That's not my girl. Yes, I know it's hard. I miss you, too. But you can always talk to me and I will always be there. I will always be there."*

Suzanne: *Okay. We're going to end with Victoria to help wrap things up.* [To Bill:] *Now about this book* [i.e., *Victoria: A Love Story*]. *Something about you're struggling with the ending.*

*I was just thinking about that yesterday. But I think I know now.*

*Yes. You're dotting the i's and crossing the t's and it's going to be so perfect. Her heart opens up at the gift you are giving your sons. Such a wonderful legacy. There's a feeling that your tears wet the paper even though you're typing it.*

*I write with a smile on my face and tears in my eyes. I have told that to many people.*

*But she's right there with you looking over your shoulder as you write. She's right there.*

*Yes. She's my co-author.*

[Sounds of exhaling—Suzanne] *She says . . . she says, "I know you would like to write the last chapter of your life, but you have many more chapters to write. You have to be there for the boys."*

94

*Yes* [quietly].

*She's just going to keep holding your hand. Now she's striking a match for some reason. Why is she doing that?*

Pat: *We experimented with smoking on the tennis courts one night.* [Laughter] *We spent a lot of time on the tennis courts. We once went through a whole book of matches trying to get them lit.*

[More laughter]

*I don't think that's it.* [Suzanne, to Bill:] *She says, light a candle for me.*

*I was just going to say, I will light a candle for her and the flame of the candle will never go out.*

*Yes, that's it.* [Light laughter—Suzanne] *There's some memory of a skunk smell.*

Pat: *Well, yeah.*

[Laughter]

Suzanne: *She's like, don't get all serious on us here, and you got that message* [of love], *Bill. But what's with the skunk?*

Pat: *Well, I hit one when we were driving out in the country.*

*Was she with you?*

*Yes. And we tried to figure out how to get the small out of my parents' car.* [Laughter] *Which we couldn't do.*

Suzanne, to us three: *Do you see how this works? This validates everything she has said this evening that you could not otherwise prove. That's the thing.* [To Bill:] *She followed up what she just said to you with a piece of evidence that could only have come from her.*

*I know it did.*

*So, okay. Let's all hold hands again . . . I am so incredibly grateful to you all.*

We three: *We are the ones who are grateful, Suzanne.*

*I am grateful to you and to my team on the other side* [her spirit guides who helped her with this reading]. *This kind of clarity is what I had prayed for.* [To Tom, John, and Victoria:] *Just keep it coming, this sort of healing. In the days to come, let your presence be known to those who love you so very much.*

As the reading concluded and Ty began uncorking several bottles of wine, Cris, Pat, and I looked at each other with the identical thought in mind: long before any beverage or food might be served, this was far and away the best party any of us had ever attended, or could ever hope to attend.

# Chapter 9

## Spirit Presence Redux

In her seminal work, *Love Never Dies* (Hay House, August 2014), renowned relationship therapist, author, and "Ask Dr. Love" media personality Dr. Jamie Turndorf writes about her spiritual reconnection with her beloved husband, Emile Jean Pin, a former Jesuit priest and scholar whom the Dalai Lama once publicly honored as "one of the fifty people of all time who was one with God." There are many ways to reconnect with the spirit of a deceased loved one, Dr. Turndorf asserts in her latest book, because the spirit, once freed of its earthly vessel, has the power to signal its presence to us by influencing the material world in an infinite variety of ways.

On one occasion, shortly after her husband's death, she tried to fax his death certificate, together with a cover letter, to Verizon to remove him from their joint account. Although earlier in the day she had faxed several multipage documents without incident, on this occasion, when she pressed the "send" button, the cover letter transmitted but the death certificate did not. She tried several more times with the same result.

Suddenly the thought popped into her mind: Jean is trying to tell me he's not gone!

The next day she took the cover letter and death certificate to her lawyer's office to fax the documents from there. But when two legal secretaries tried to fax the documents, the same thing happened: the cover letter went through but the certificate did not. "It's as though your husband is telling you he's not gone," they told Dr. Turndorf.

The next morning she again tried to fax the cover letter and death certificate from her home fax machine. Again the cover letter went through but the death certificate did not. This time she said aloud, "Jean, you keep preventing your death certificate from faxing because I keep forgetting that you're still here with me. If I promise to try to remember, will you let the fax go through now?"

As she canceled the fax, she simultaneously felt a "tidal wave of love" pouring into her. When she again tried faxing the documents, they both went through without a hitch.

⌐⌐

Although no spirit has shown its presence to me by manipulating my fax machine, I have had similar experiences involving the manipulation of my computer.

When my sons and I moved from our home in Minneapolis into an apartment in Wayzata, I was granted the master suite because (a) I am the father and that title should come with some advantages, and (b) I needed to set up my office in my bedroom to avoid disturbing anyone when I arose before dawn to begin my writing/editing routine. In the middle of one night, after getting up to use the bathroom, I was lying supine on my bed staring up at the ceiling barely visible in the feeble glimmer of a nightlight. As always happens on such occasions, my thoughts drifted back to earlier years when Victoria was lying on that same bed beside me and I would take such pleasure and comfort in simply watching her sleep. As I began drifting off to sleep, I felt a warm blanket of love settle over me—one similar in effect to the "tidal wave of love" described by Dr. Turndorf in the passage above—and I said gently into the night, "I love you, Dearheart." At that very instant my computer restarted, the light from its wide screen washing the room in a soft white glow.

Although the hour was early, I did not get back to sleep that night. Yes, computers do sometimes restart automatically, for reasons that involve the internal workings of the machine when, for example, certain programs are upgraded. In my experience it happens once or twice a month. But what is the probability that it would restart at that precise moment?

Dr. Gary Schwartz, professor of psychology, medicine, neurology, psychiatry, and surgery at the University of Arizona—and director of its Laboratory for Advances in Consciousness and Health—refers to such a phenomenon as a synchronicity. In brief, a synchronicity occurs when the interaction of two (or more) unrelated events is too coincidental to be accidental. The more synchronicities in a related chain of events, he asserts, the higher the probability that these "divine coincidences" indicate a spirit presence. Such as when a computer restarts in the middle of a night immediately after an expression of love to a spirit. Which is what has happened to me—on four separate occasions. To date.

At about this same time I had a second wildlife encounter involving a possible spirit presence, this time in the behavior of a little red bird.

While living in Wayzata with my two older sons, I was alone for most days during the week. Both sons worked in the Twin Cities—one at the state house in St. Paul and the other at Methodist Hospital in Minneapolis—so I was left to do my writing and editing in relative peace and quiet. The month was April, I believe, because the weather was beginning to warm up nicely (meaning, in Minnesota, that even nighttime temperatures hover above zero) and the first inklings of spring were everywhere in evidence.

On one Monday morning I took my usual ten o'clock break from work to walk from my bedroom-office into the kitchen to brew another cup of coffee. As I walked into the living room with the coffee I noticed, through a large window on its south-facing side, a little red bird perched on a branch of a substantial forsythia bush whose tiny buds were revealing their first splashes of yellow. As I sat down in a chair, the bird flew over from the branch and lit on a windowsill, where it stood rooted in place watching me. It was still there a few minutes later when I got up and returned to my desk.

I thought nothing of it that morning, and only a little about it the following morning when the bird repeated the same evolutions as on the previous day. However, on the third morning, when the bird again flew over to the windowsill when it saw me enter the living room, it received my full attention. Acting on an impulse, I arose from the chair and took several tentative steps toward the window, until the space between us was perhaps four feet.

Under normal circumstances a bird would be startled by the approach of a human and fly away. Not this bird. Not on that day. It stood its ground, watching me with the same trancelike expression I had noticed on the two rabbits. Acting on another impulse, I mouthed the words "I love you" at the bird. After I did so, the bird started pecking its beak against the windowpane. After perhaps five seconds that seemed more like five minutes, the bird stopped, took one final long look at me, and then flew off, its message delivered.

I never saw that bird again.

⁓

We all have dreams, arguably every night. During the last four centuries a great deal of time, energy, and money have been invested in oneirology—the study of the meaning of dreams—as well as dream analysis, which studies the physiology of the dreaming process. Yet, although enough books have been written on the subject to fill a library, what lies behind the content and purpose of dreams remains largely a mystery to the broad medical community.

During the past two years, based on what I have read and especially on what I have experienced, I have come to believe that dreams can serve as a platform for spirit visitations. When such a phenomenon occurs, it is not a dream you remember vaguely when you wake up, recalling only disjointed bits of fantasy about what was involved where and with whom. Rather, it is as Dr. Turndorf describes, as though a voice calls out in the middle of a dream, "We interrupt this broadcast to bring you a special announcement!" and everything and everyone in the dream is transformed from a murky gray into living Technicolor, and even the most minute details involving people and place become shockingly clear.

To date, I have experienced two such dreams, both of them involving a bridge. The example I include in this chapter is the more comprehensive of the two, although no more vivid in its detail.

In the dream, Victoria and I had flown to California to visit the graduate school of physician assistant studies at which our son had recently been accepted. While in real life this had happened—in February 2014—Victoria and I appeared in the dream as we had during the early years of marriage in the late 1970s. In other words, we were in our early thirties, not in our middle sixties as we would appear today. At the airport we picked up a rental car, I got behind the wheel with 20/20 vision, and we started driving along a wide boulevard toward town. To this day I can still recall in intricate detail how the buildings on the side of the road were constructed and what colors they were painted. I can also vividly recall the palm trees and shrubbery lining the road and sidewalks, and the make of other cars (all of modern vintage) and the style of clothes the pedestrians were wearing.

"What street are we looking for?" I asked Victoria, who was studying a city map.

"Commonwealth Avenue," she replied. [Although in real life our son's school is not located on Commonwealth Avenue, the apartment he was soon to visit and subsequently rent is located on a street of that name.] "I think I see it up ahead. We take a right on it and then go another few miles down the road. That's where the school is."

"Are we on time for our appointment with the dean?" I asked her.

Victoria glanced at her wristwatch. "Yes. We still have thirty minutes. We should be there in plenty of time."

I took the right on Commonwealth, and as we followed it through some lovely Southern California landscapes, Victoria and I chattered away about any number of topics in the same easy, comfortable, loving manner we had so enjoyed during our thirty-four years of marriage. Suddenly she turned to look back.

"I think we just missed our exit," she said.

I glanced in the rearview mirror. "You're right," I said. "Well, let's see where this road takes us."

Where that road took us was onto a narrow, one-lane, one-way bridge that seemed to stretch to eternity. Another bridge of similar construction ran parallel to it, its traffic going in the opposite direction. All around us was an unruffled turquoise sea on which a treasure trove of white diamonds sparkled brightly beneath the warm California sun.

After driving along the bridge for some time I said, "I'm afraid we're going to be very late for our appointment."

In reply, Victoria flashed me one of her glorious smiles. "So what? We're together now. That's all that matters, isn't it?"

I returned her smile. "Yes, my love. It is."

Eventually we saw land looming on the horizon, and as we approached it, I went slack-jawed. Never had I seen such a beautiful and dazzling place. The combined talents of the best writers in history could not begin to do justice to the glory, wonder, and stunning splendor of this sun-drenched haven awash in the most brilliant and eye-catching colors imaginable, from the rich panoply of flowers rooted to the sodden earth to the breathtaking splendor of deciduous and coniferous trees towering into the cerulean blue sky.

"My God, this is magnificent," I gasped, utterly awestruck as my eyes absorbed the ethereal majesty of it all. "We have got to come back here."

"We will," Victoria assured me. "But right now we need to get back to the school (of life)."

Reluctantly I turned the car around and we headed back to the mainland. After an indeterminable span of time we arrived at the school, parked the car, and walked briskly to the administrative building, where a receptionist politely ushered us into the dean's office.

As we shook hands with the finely attired and spectacled academician, I apologized profusely for our being so late to the appointment.

The dean gave me a quizzical look and glanced at his watch. "Mr. Hammond," he said unequivocally, "you need not apologize. You are not late. In fact you are several minutes early."

At that moment I woke up. I so wanted to go back to sleep, to return to the bliss of being reunited with my wife, but I was unable to. So I got up and sat down at my computer with the intent of transcribing every detail of the dream. But as I sat there staring at screen and keyboard, I typed nothing at all. Because I realized I didn't need to. The events and descriptions depicted in that dream were so ingrained in my brain that I could not possibly forget them. And I haven't. Not one detail.

A few weeks later (a meaningless detail, really, since time as we understand it has no relevance on the other side), I received the following email from Pat Leavell, who has also researched the subject of dreams in her attempt to reconnect with John. Her email is presented below. I have not changed a word of it. Nor would I ever want to.

Bill, my sister Lynn just called me. Last night she dreamt of VICKI!!!!!!!!!!!!!!!!!!!!! Now Lynn is just 50 years old, so her memories of Vicki are from many years ago, when Vicki would have been in her early 20s. Anyway, Lynn was trying to get through a forest of trees. She was trying to get through for some reason, and she saw that there were several figures wearing black cloaks with hoods, and she knew instinctively that these were bad creatures and she had to avoid them. So she was sneaking around, hiding behind trees and trying to go forward with not much success. All of a sudden, she saw another figure wearing a white cloak with a hood that was not over her head. She realized that it was Vicki. Vicki was BEAUTIFUL!!!! Her hair was honey brown, so thick and just above her shoulders. Her hair curled under her chin a little bit. She was wearing those over-sized glasses that were so popular in the 70s, and her face was glowing, smiling, perfect white teeth, and was absolutely beautiful. She told Lynn (not with her voice, but with her thoughts) that she would take care of her, and that she would get her safely through the forest. Lynn said that she looked so stunning, not sick, but full of joy, and health and love was just radiating off of her. She said that she woke up right then, and she knew that she was safe, that Vicki was going to help her, and that she was supposed to tell me so that I would tell you that she was healthy and was all around you and your boys, me and her and everyone that she loved in her lifetime. Lynn said it was a visitation, not a dream, as the picture was so vivid, and she has complete recall of it, not like a dream that fades away in a few minutes.

So—here's the message from your beloved wife. She's more than okay, she's perfect in every way and she's watching over you and the boys, helping you through all those forests you face every day, and keeping you safely away from the bad guys!

How's that for a Wednesday afternoon present????? It's given to you with love.

Bless you, Pat. Your present is received with love by me and with appreciation by scores of others who now better understand the devotion and comfort and protection provided by a loved one in spirit form, and how the reach of a spirit's love goes beyond a spouse or another immediate family member to include the entire circle of love the spirit had known while in human form.

⌒

Not long after receiving that email from Pat, I received an email from Suzanne Giesemann. Attached to it was chapter 1 of *Wolf's Message*, the manuscript she had just begun writing that was destined to become an instant bestseller on Amazon. "Would you mind taking a quick look at it," she asked, "and give me your honest first impression?"

A "quick look" turned into a slow read—for me, the clearest indication that I am taken with a manuscript—as I became enthralled with the text and the first of its key

messages delivered by an incredible young man with the
nickname of Wolf, now in spirit form. Whenever you ask
an editor to read anything, you do so at your peril, because
it is almost certain to incur the attention of a blue pencil.
So I retuned the draft of the chapter to Suzanne with a few
proposed light edits—a suggested new turn of phrase, a
different choice of words, the insertion or (more commonly)
deletion of an adverb; in other words the same sort of
copyedits that Mindy Conner, my editor in North Carolina,
performs on my manuscripts—and asked her to please send
me chapter 2 as soon as it was ready. Which she did. And I
edited that chapter as well, in the same way.

"Bill," she wrote in a subsequent email, "you're obviously
my editor, and I want you to be. But I feel awkward about it
because we haven't discussed compensation."

"Nor will we," I wrote back immediately. "I can place a
value on my editing services, Suzanne, but I cannot place
a value on what you have given to me and to those dear to
me. It is a priceless gift. It is, in fact, the *ultimate* gift."

My email may have addressed the matter, but it did not
settle it. Suzanne had yet another gift in store for me, one
that involved another close encounter with my beloved
wife in spirit form, this time in the company of my deceased
father and mother, as well as the spirit of my sister Diana.

## Chapter 10

## Reading 3

As was true in their visit in September of 2013, Ty and Suzanne had a specific reason for traveling to Minneapolis the following Memorial Day weekend. Again they wanted to visit with close friends, and again Suzanne had a speaking engagement, this time at the Unity Christ Church, located approximately a mile from our old home in Golden Valley, which in turn is three miles from downtown Minneapolis. Once again Cris flew up from Scottsdale for the occasion. Pat Leavell wanted to come, but she had recently sold her house in Nebraska and was deep in the process of moving into a new home.

For Cris, there was an added incentive for traveling north for the week besides escaping the mounting heat in Arizona for the glory of the three-week season that Minnesotans refer to as "spring." In addition to seeing Suzanne and Ty again, Suzanne had offered her a third reading with Tom on Friday morning, just as she had offered me a third reading with Victoria on Saturday morning. Those offers were impossible not to accept.

Although Suzanne's speaking engagement was scheduled for 7:30 on the Friday evening of the three-day
weekend—not the best timing for a public presentation
but the only date available—the spacious room was filled
to capacity long before she was scheduled to begin her
address. Cris, my son Churchill, and I arrived at 7:10 to
find only a few empty chairs scattered here and there
about the room. When I happened to mention to one of
the friendly hosts of the event that I served as Suzanne's
editor, she leapt into action and within no time we three
were seated comfortably together. Yes, it does help to
know people in high places!

As usual, at the end of her three-hour address that
included a tsunami of questions, the audience rose as one
(those who were seated, that is; many people in the room
had stood for the entire presentation) to give Suzanne a
sustained ovation. It was nearly eleven by the time we left
the church, too late to enjoy a glass of wine with Suzanne
and Ty. But we were not forlorn. Cris had had an excellent reading that morning, one that had her smiling as she
emerged from the Giesemanns' coach, and I knew without
question that I had an equally meaningful experience await-
ing me the next morning.

I met Suzanne at her campsite at eleven, and as Cris, my
sons, and Ty drove off to a nearby town for a cup of coffee, Suzanne and I sat down across from each other in the
coach. This was our first one-on-one reading in the physical presence of each other, and I felt a surge of emotion as
we joined hands and Suzanne offered a prayer of gratitude
and love to the Source of All That Is. After flipping on the

tape recorder to tape the session, she closed her eyes and held out her hands toward me, as if in a blessing.

*I'm waiting for Victoria to step in—I know she's already here—and blend so completely with me so that I disappear and you can have this time with Bill.* [Sounds of exhaling—Suzanne] Okay. *The first thing I hear is, "Oh my sweetheart, I love you so much."*

*Oh, dear God . . .*

*And the book* [Victoria: A Love Story] *is beautiful. And we wrote it together.*

*Yes, we did.*

*She says she had to nudge you a few times. I don't understand that, but she says you would understand that.*

*I do understand that.*

*And she woke you up a few times at night as well.*

*Yes.*

*A sweet and devilish laugh. No, not devilish; a playful laugh that you didn't mind.*

*No.*

*While I was meditating, she shared with me that you were handling something of hers early this morning. It was not the book; it was something else. Did you touch something of hers this morning?*

*Yes.*

*Okay. One of you is having trouble with the throat.*

*Yes. Churchill is.*

*She loved nursing all of you. It seems like there was little pain with childbirth, less than normal. Is that true?*

*That is true. She had little pain compared to most women. With all three.* [All three sons were born within several hours of our arriving at Brigham & Women's Hospital in Boston. After our first son was born, Victoria's obstetrician quipped that with our next pregnancy we should have a helicopter standing by on our lawn in suburban Boston.]

*Yes. That is what she is saying. Beautiful. Okay, she says, "There's your evidence. Now, get on with it."* [Laughter—Suzanne and me] . . . *All right.* [Sounds of exhaling—Suzanne] . . . *So powerful. She says you have made her out to be an angel.*

*She is an angel.*

*She's bowing her head, as if humble, but she is very pleased.* [See appendix B to see what Suzanne was likely visualizing.]

*She would bow her head* [whenever she was praised].

*Yes, like a blushing bride. But inside, it's nice.* [Light laughter—Suzanne]

*Yes. She is my angel.*

*She says if I open my eyes and look over at you, you'll still have your* [wedding] *ring on.*

*Yes. Always.*

[Laughter—Suzanne] *And she says, "My husband is just like the character in his books* [Richard Cutler in the Cutler Family Chronicles] *if another woman comes on to him."* [Like Richard, since marrying the love of my life I have had—and will continue to have—no interest in pursuing a romantic involvement with another woman. However, I am blessed to have many female friends, each of whom I love dearly.]

*Yes.*

*Brooks . . . There is a sense that he is going to do very well in the P.A.* [physician's assistant] *program. There's also a sense that he is feeling a little over his head. Do you know if that's true?*

*There's no question that he did feel overwhelmed in the process of getting in.* [And now that he is in, like all medical school students he is at times feeling totally overwhelmed by the breadth and depth of his studies.]

*And she wants Churchill not to give up on his political science focus. And she takes me to D.C. and the State Department. Did he talk with Ty about the State Department?*

*I don't know. He and I have certainly talked about it. He's taking the civil service exam next month.*

*Next month, Bill?*

*Yes. In three weeks.*

*Wow. Because I'm seeing the State Department as clear as day. Good. That's good. That Harrison. There's nothing he can't do. And there's a gung-ho attitude about him.* [Laughter—Suzanne] *She's talking about energy, energy, energy. He must have been very energetic as a child.*

*Yes. Very.*

*Yes, and she's showing me him going up and over obstacles as on an obstacle course. And he's a motivating force to those around him.*

*Yes.*

*Okay. You must always go and sit by the lake, because she says she always sits there beside you.*

*Oh, dear God.*

*And you just talk.*

*Yes, I talk out loud to her. I do it every day.* [If passers-by think I'm a babbling old fool while I'm sitting there, so be it.]

*Just the two of you.*

*Yes.*

*Oh, oh, she says this morning's message from Sanaya*

*is from her. Wait until you see it. She says it's appropriate
because you so often sit by the lake and look out over the water.*

I will look for that [message].

*That happens a lot. Whoever is part of the morning's
reading comes up in Sanaya's message of the day. There's a
feeling that there is much concern and yet no concern—there's
a paradox here—when it comes to money. It's as though you
worry about money, but then have no worry when you spend it.
Does that make sense?*

It makes absolute sense.

*Okay. She's showing me a snow shovel and then her hand
goes to her lower back. Did you have back problems?*

Always when I shoveled snow. I would come back in with
back pain.

*You know, it's amazing. She's laughing about that, but
in a positive way. She had such a positive attitude about
everything.*

She always did. That was her very nature.

*She's showing me a birthday cake with one candle on it, as
though it was a private joke that you didn't want to admit your
age and made a joke about it.*

[Laughter—me] *There are so many ramifications about
that [statement] that apply to what she just said. I know
exactly what she's saying.* [For one thing, Victoria was per-
petually twenty-two years old, and that became a standing
joke in our family, especially after our oldest son turned
twenty-three.]

*Oh, my God, Bill, it's so clear. She's nodding her head and
laughing, as if to say, "Yes, yes, of course he does. You are in
my head and I am in yours."*

*Yes. And in my heart.*

*Okay. Oh, wow.* She says, "There is nothing I liked better than to sit beside you and hold your hand. If I could have gotten into your skin, I would have done so, and you the same. We could walk for hours on the beach and not have to say a word. Just listen to the birds and hear their squawking and watch the sun rise or set, it didn't matter. We are the truest example of two souls being one."

*Yes. So true.*

*I know you would have taken the sickness out of her and put it in your own body.*

Yes [quietly].

*But it was not to be, she says. Oh, my, she says, "Do you realize how many lives you will touch now that your writing has taken a different turn? You have so many followers already and this new venture will extend that number ever more greatly." Okay. All right. You have a nightly ritual before going to bed. You talk to her and you light a candle to her. Is that right?*

Yes. I light [an electric] candle to her every evening. It's by my bedroom window next to her urn [handmade by her sons to hold her ashes]. That's what I was touching this morning.

*Yes. That's what she's showing me. Now she's showing me a necklace. You two were going out and the necklace broke and you fixed it like you fixed everything else. Is this a memory?*

Yes. That did happen some years ago. She had a pearl necklace and it broke and I tried to get it back on her. And I succeeded, so I did fix it; this time, at least.

[Laughter—Suzanne and me]

*I don't know if this was the occasion, but she's showing me you speaking at some function. I was not aware of you doing public speaking.*

*I've done some.* [To promote my books. I believe she is referring here to the speech I made to Harrison's high school—all 450 students and faculty—as the school's "author of the year." She loved that speech.]

*And she's saying you were so eloquent and she is so proud of the way you express yourself verbally and on paper. She's taking me back to the hospital. There were some around her who were hardened to their work, but there was something about the energy in her room, so much love in her room, that everyone really looked forward to caring for her because of that.*

*There is no question of that. She did that* [made that impression on people] *all her life, but it was never more apparent than when she was in the hospital.* [A nurse stationed on the fifth floor who cared for Victoria when she was first admitted came down to the oncology floor to visit with her almost every day until the end, even after Victoria had slipped into a coma.]

*And there was a male doctor who is listening very carefully to you. I don't know if you were trying to get him to do something, but you wanted him to listen to you.*

*Yes.* [Victoria had a team of four doctors, one of whom was male. That doctor wanted to transfer Victoria from Methodist Hospital to a local nursing home, which I knew was not what Victoria wanted. In an emotional appeal during a meeting with all four doctors, I finally convinced him to allow her to be placed in the care of the hospital's hospice center. The other three doctors agreed with me.]

*Your father is here. I don't know if Cris told you that he came* [to her reading] *yesterday.*

Yes, she did.

*I know this* [reading] *is all about Victoria, but he's pointing at the book* [Victoria: A Love Story] *and saying, "Well done, son."*

Thank you, Dad.

*I always loved her, he says.*

I know you did.

*The book is a real tribute to her and to us as well.* [Suzanne, to me:] *There are things that came out yesterday with your sister that tell a different story than what you tell in the book. But he's thanking you for respecting the family's dignity and honor.* [Dad, to me:] *We* [meaning he and my mother] *always tried our best. It's a matter of upbringing that passes on from one generation to another.*

Yes.

*We always tried to come from a place of love.*

Yes [quietly].

*We were formal and strict at times.* [Suzanne, to me:] *Does that make sense?*

Completely. I know exactly what he is saying.

*Okay. Your sister is thanking you for being there for her.*

Diana?

Yes.

*I was there at the end* [in 2008, in a hospice center in Asheville, North Carolina]. *So was Cris. I tried to always be there for her. Such a wonderful sister.*

*She really looked up to you. She's showing me a guitar. Did you play the guitar?*

*Yes, but not very well.* [In fact, I was horrible at it.] *But I tried hard, and she always liked that I did.*

*Okay. Excellent. I see Victoria standing nearby and she wants to talk with you, but she wants to give you this time* [with your parents and sister].

*That's wonderful.*

*Your sister says that she is finally at peace, as if she were not at peace here in this life. Always self-critical, self-defacing, never satisfied with herself. But she's now learning to love herself, finally.*

*Good. Because she should.*

*She didn't let others love her. She didn't let others in. But she always loved you.*

*Oh, dear God. I love you too, Di-Di.*

*Okay. Getting back to your wife . . . No, we're still with Diana. She says that Victoria is the best thing that has ever happened to the whole family.*

[Choking sounds—me] *I can't disagree.*

*Your mother . . . There's a sense that she was a strong woman, not always silent, and that's the funny thing. She would know when it was appropriate to be quiet, which is why she has been standing off to the side. But, oh, there were times when you could not stop her from talking.*

*Yes.*

*There's this quiet dignity of knowing when and when not to speak. She just wants you to know that she's here and that she loves you with all her heart and that she is so proud of you.*

*Dear God.*

*There's something about scarves.*

*She wore scarves a lot.*

*Not a winter scarf.*

Right.

*Very beautiful ones. Such a dignified, classy lady.*

Yes, all of those things.

*And a perfectionist when it comes to entertaining and decorating. Is that true?*

Yes. She was an artist as well.

*And she would be dressed to the nines and would need to sit up straight with correct posture. A very regal bearing.*

Just so.

*Your wife was like this, but she could also get down and dirty. [Laughter—Suzanne and me] Yes, I see your wife in coveralls, in blue jeans.*

Yes.

*But your mother—*

No way.

*—would find that beneath her. She would not want to get dirt under her fingernails.*

That's all true.

*Whereas Victoria would love the feel of the earth.*

Absolutely. [Victoria loved planting flowers, fruits, and vegetables.]

*So out of respect, she [my mother] says, we have stayed in the background until now.*

*You are never in the background.*

*But we are all so proud of you. We know you are feeling better now. We have all tried to help you through these hard times and take on your pain. Just as you tried to do for your beloved wife. She is like a daughter to us. We are taking good care of her, and she is doing the same for us. It's not like it is here* [in the physical realm]. *We just get to love each other and we feel it so fully. And that is what we give you now and with every breath you take. We are so proud of you, son. We know you could never fail. None of you children could, and you are all so different. And she says that we may not have dealt with you the way you individually would have wanted, but you were the most adjusted of the three. That's a human judgment, but you were the one most comfortable in your own skin. But we know that you all know that we did the best we could, and we are happy with the knowledge that you know that.*

We do. Wow . . . that goes to the heart.

*Your father is nodding, and there's such a feeling of peace with all of them.*

Good. I'm so glad. I love them all.

*Okay. Victoria says, "It's now time for you and me."*

[Laughter—Suzanne and me]

*Both of you. The feel of your skin together was magical, electric. Everything about you clicked.*

Yes. So true.

*You must not have been able to tie a tie.*

[Laughter—me] Yes. *She's got it. A bowtie.* [I never could get the hang of it, so to speak, no matter how hard I tried. So I finally gave up trying—and tying.]

[Laughter—Suzanne] *She's laughing now. "You just lack style," she says. It sounds insulting, but it's not meant that way.*

I understand.

*This is a joke with you.*

It is. I totally understand. [And so would my sons, who in

recent years have ribbed me unmercifully about my lack of style when it comes to clothes.]

*She's showing me a palette and she's spilling paint on it. Does that make sense to you?*

Yes. [Several months after Victoria passed on, I was in a grocery store with my three sons, standing still in a daze. I was dressed in a pumpkin-orange T-shirt, a knee-length yellow bathing suit, a red sailing cap, and white socks with beige boat shoes. My oldest son, Churchill, approached me at one point, set his hands on his hips as he looked me up and down, and said, "Dad, you just don't give a damn, do you?" That story has made the rounds over the years and has given delight to many people.]

*Okay. Oh, she is showing me a small box, Bill. It's like a cash box or a box full of memories. There's something import-ant in there. A document is in there.*

*Hmm . . . I have several boxes of photographs and memorabilia.*

*That's not it. Is there a certificate you recently looked at?*

*Yes, there is. It's our marriage certificate. I did that only a week ago.* [I was searching for something in the bottom drawer of my desk when I came across that box.]

*That is very cool. How many people do that? Oh, and she says, "See? I'm with you always, whenever you think of me. And you're not keeping me from anything. Didn't I always do anything just to be with you?"*

Yes.

*"And I'm still doing it. I'm not that busy. Ha-ha." And she's still creating art.*

Good.

*I don't know how that works. I really don't. But she's doing it.
Wonderful.*

*And she loves music. She shows me you two dancing and
there is no place she would rather be than in your arms. The
boys may laugh at that, but they so enjoyed seeing you two love
each other so much.*

That is true.

*One of them was a really good baseball player.*

They all were. Brooks was captain of his high school baseball team.

*And you didn't miss many games.*

I never missed a game [that any of them played in].

*Did someone play the violin at some point?*

Brooks played the cello. He took lessons because his mother
made him do it.

[Laughter—Suzanne and me]

*She's telling me that that there is a natural competition
among the boys, but there is a supportiveness of each other that
is unheralded. Interesting word.*

I agree with her.

*And each has cheered on the others in life, and they love you
so, and she loves them and is so grateful to them for helping
you through this.*

So true. They did help me. Each one of them is a gift from
God to us both.

*She knows your hearts were cut out and she knows that was
a double burden for them. [Her death] was the worst thing
they have had to bear, but despite that, they supported you
more than you could support them. And she is so awed by that,
but not surprised by it.*

*All so true.*

*The blending is so complete, she says, "I want to wrap you in my arms and hold you." But she says you do that every day.*

Yes, we do.

*Wow. Now she is showing me a samurai sword. Do you recognize that?*

No, I don't.

*Ask Churchill about it, okay?*

I will. [When I did ask him later that day, he reminded me that years ago in Hingham he was given as a gift a wooden replica of a samurai sword. He displayed it in his room for years. I had completely forgotten about it. Obviously, Victoria had not.]

*She says that the whole process [of writing the book] was cleansing and cathartic as we walked down Memory Lane together. She brought many memories to [your] mind that you had completely forgotten about, and that's how you knew she was with you—because she always had the better memory when she was here and you couldn't have done this without her. [Laughter—Suzanne and me]*

True.

[Laughter—Suzanne] *Bill, I just asked for evidence and she says that there's something going on with your toenail.*

Yes. I have a cut toenail. [Just a few days earlier my son Brooks had commented on it.]

*Okay . . . Oh, my God. Wow. Now she's saying, "There is no detail so small that it gets past me. Didn't I always tell you that I'm the detail person?"*

She always did. Dear God.

*Yes, and she's in your thoughts always, because you two are of one mind.*

Yes.

*Flying right beside you. There's a sense that you're going somewhere and you already have your tickets.*

Yes. To Scottsdale.

*And you have the tickets?*

Brooks and I are planning to buy them this weekend. We just decided that yesterday.

*Okay. Perfect. Because she is going to fly right beside you, like an angel. Oh, my goodness, she says, "I mean that literally. There is no place that you go that I am not with you."*

Oh, God.

*She says, "What more can I say?" This is a special time because you have the evidence that you don't really need anymore and she is grateful for that. She is in your heart, always.*

I know she is.

*And she is so pleased that you are all together this weekend and that you can celebrate life. Because that's all there is. Life and love.*

Yes, my darling. That is all there is. Life and love. With you. For eternity.

## Chapter 11

## Reflections

Despite the overwhelming preponderance of evidence embedded in the three readings—evidence supported by more ethereal indications of spirit presence—many skeptics will debunk everything in this book, claiming that the readings were somehow "rigged" and the emanations of spirit presence are nothing more than odd coincidences. That's all right. I understand. Like Captain Ty Giesemann—indeed, like Commander Suzanne Giesemann herself—I would have counted myself among those skeptics not so long ago.

Besides, I didn't write this book with that audience in mind. I am not out to "convert" anyone or to convince anyone of anything. My purpose in writing this book is simply to share my spiritual journey with those individuals who are open to the prospect that their loved ones not only live on after death but also remain with them 24/7. And they are there to help comfort, protect, and heal their loved ones. If this book helps but one living soul find the peace and serenity that I have found from coming to understand this greater reality, then it has been well worth the writing.

What follows are lessons I have learned and conclusions I have drawn as a result of taking a far-flung spiritual quest that started with Victoria's passing and shifted into high gear six months later, at the time of my first reading. These lessons and conclusions are not meant to be profound or in any way earth shattering. Certainly I do not represent myself as a religious teacher or one in possession of unique insights into either religion or spirituality. (Books written by individuals who do possess those divine gifts are included in the list in Appendix A.) I, too, am in the process of learning; my spiritual journey just recently started. These observations are therefore those of an "ordinary Joe" (or an "ordinary Bill," if you prefer) who has long been struggling with the same cosmic issues that confront every human being who has ever inhabited this planet.

Perhaps the most immediate question to address is what all this means, to me, about my own death—and by extension the death of every human. Certainly the transition of believing in the spirit realm to knowing such a realm exists puts a different perspective on death. As a result of what I learned during the first reading—a conviction reinforced by the second and third readings—I no longer fear death in any shape or form. Victoria has promised me that when my time comes, as it does for us all, she will be the first to greet me on the other side. What in heaven's name is there to fear in such a promise made by the love of my life?

That is not to say that I am seeking to end my life prematurely in order to join my wife in Paradise. Although I do not wish to extend my life beyond a certain threshold of quality, as I have duly recorded in a living will, I do not seek to die before my time. I have three sons whom I love dearly (just as their mother does) and who will continue to need the material and emotional support of their father for as long as I am able to give it. Because life is a gift from God, it is to be cherished and honored, and used to the good of humankind whenever possible. I am hopeful that this book will contribute in some small way to that common good.

Besides, however long I may have to live as a spiritual being temporarily in physical form on this earth, it is, as we are taught in Bible studies, but a blink of an eye to those inhabiting the spirit realm. Eternity is a long time. And knowing that I will be spending eternity with Victoria and with all those I love in the past, present, and future inspires a depth of comfort and anticipation and joy that defies adequate verbal explanation.

~

On a related issue, what I have discovered in my journey is that the old adage "Time heals all wounds" is simply not true. Yes, I am feeling better these days. That is due, in part, to the meaningful life I lead, one that I am fortunate to share with loving friends and family. It is also due to my involvement with several causes that honor my wife's life and legacy. Perhaps most important, it is due to the knowledge that Victoria wants me to be happy where I am because she is so happy where she is—and where we will both be happy together someday.

Having said that, time will never heal the pain of losing

her physical presence. Time can only numb that pain. It
will remain with me in one form or another until the day
I die, at which point all pain and suffering attached to my
human body will disappear and I will be one with Victoria
and with all those I love who have gone before me and who
will come after me. It will be a time of eternal joy.

Of course, what is profiled above defines the one-sided
nature of the grieving process. When our loved ones leave
the physical realm to return home to the spiritual realm, we
grieve not for them, but for us.

⌒

For me, death is somewhere in the future. What, then, of
the present? What else have I learned so far during my
journey toward spiritual awakening about what is important
in my life three years after my Victoria died? Allow me to
answer that question initially with an insight into what I
now find unimportant.

Like many young couples, when Victoria and I were
first married we became enmeshed in the web of materialism that so captivates our capitalist society. We wanted a
new car, a vacation to an exotic locale, a dinner out at a
preferred restaurant, the latest technological innovation.
Today, my perspective has changed somewhat. Such objects
and dreams have their place in our lives, but they do not
represent what is truly important. The Bible and other
more worldly works have a great deal to say on the subject
of materialism, and there is no need for me to echo those
words except to emphasize that they contain universal
truths. For most people, the death of one dearly beloved has

a way of putting everything into proper perspective, at least until the tides of pain and grief have subsided. Of this I am certain: it is not of such material things and possessions that our lives will ultimately be judged, either by others or by ourselves.

For me today, nothing—*nothing*—is more meaningful than to sit quietly by a body of water with a cup of hot coffee or iced tea in hand and reflect on the wealth of heart-warming memories that so imbue my body, mind, and spirit. However long my physical life may endure, I will never be able to adequately express my gratitude to God, the Source and Creator of All That Is, for the manifold blessings of those gifts that have been bestowed upon me and mine. In the shining light of that greater reality, who wins a college or pro football game, which political party rules our government, or what new gizmo Apple introduces to the buying public no longer seems all that important. Life will go on, regardless. And our journey on this earth will end someday, regardless. We are all terminal. If I once embraced the adage that "he who dies with the most toys wins," today I see it as a sad and empty promise. The more accurate perspective, I have come to believe, is that "he who dies with the fullest heart wins." Perhaps my gaining that perspective signifies that somewhere along the path of my journey I have begun to grow spiritually. I hope it does.

I know Victoria's spirit now resides in a "place of light" in which she is supremely happy and at peace. And as she told me in the second reading, she wants me to be happy and at peace, too. Which I am, whenever I think of her and the many blissful memories we share.

Since her death my past has become my present—and
my future.

⌒

Because I have not heard or read of evil spirits or demons
anywhere along my spiritual journey, I no longer believe in
them. Certainly there are "bad guys" out there who com-
mit unfathomable acts of violence against innocent men,
women and children, but these "demons" are not controlled
by evil spirits. They are controlled by the free will we all
possess as physical beings to do either good or bad. No
doubt, in some peoples' minds free will has gone awry. But
despite such perpetrators of iniquity, good will ultimately
prevail because God is infinite power, infinite wisdom, and
infinite love, and God is everywhere.

Nor do I believe in hell as a physical place. We all came
from the spirit world and we are all destined to return there,
eventually. It is our one true home. I do, however, believe in
a personal version of "hell" after death that is self-imposed
by remorse over evil deeds one committed while living on
the physical plane. Hell can also be defined as being denied
God's love (i.e., denied access to the spirit realm), if only
temporarily.

By the same token, I no longer think of God as a venge-
ful old man with a long white beard presiding over His
kingdom from some mountaintop high in the heavens, forever on the lookout for sinners who sooner or later will feel
the full weight of His wrath and judgment. That Sunday
school vision of God is best left to clergy and congregants
stuck in ancient teachings of the Church. Today, I perceive

God as neither man nor woman nor human in any shape or form. Rather, I perceive God as a supreme power that exists everywhere in the Universe (defined as everyone and everything in the physical realm plus everyone and everything in the spirit realm) and is always good. As spiritual beings temporarily living in this physical realm, we are all of One Mind with our God, from whose image and essence we are created. The love of God, therefore, manifests everywhere and is unconditional, regardless of how we might use or abuse the free will with which we are all endowed.

Nor does God micromanage either our lives or the many diverse forces—good and bad—that pervade our lives. We who are of One Mind with God reveal His love for us in how we, as humans, respond to those forces. For example, God had no desire to devastate Louisiana with the hurricane that killed nearly two thousand people and left countless others homeless. He had nothing to do with the formation of that storm off the west coast of Africa or the course it followed over the warm waters of the Atlantic Ocean and Gulf of Mexico. That storm did not manifest His feelings about the people who lived there. Rather, God's love for us and for all living things is manifested in the human response to the suffering caused by that storm.

I have no proof to offer for what is profiled in the above paragraphs. It is simply what I have come to know in my heart as Truth.

⌒

How does/should a "spiritual awakening" affect one's religious beliefs—by which I mean the beliefs promulgated by a conventional church set within a physical structure, whatever its faith or denomination? After all, if an individual comes to the same realizations I have that (1) the spirit realm exists and is our true home, (2) we as spiritual beings are all destined to return home, and (3) any individual on this earthly plane can communicate directly with the spirit of a loved one without the sanction or intervention of a priest or another of a holy order, does the church still have a meaningful role to play in that individual's spiritual growth?

The question is apparently being answered with a resounding "no" by the legions of people in North America, Europe, and Australia who no longer attend church services on a regular basis but who nevertheless yearn to explore and manifest their own spirituality outside the confines of a conventional church or the dogma of a certain denomination. A recent study revealed, for example, that these days more people—including those of the younger generations—tend to meditate and pray more frequently than they did, say, twenty years ago. And because of declining numbers in Christian and Jewish congregations, and the aging of those congregations, these institutions are being hard-pressed financially. A church or synagogue has salaries and bills to pay just like any other ongoing concern, and since its revenue base largely depends on contributions pledged by members of the congregation who can afford to write generous checks, these bills become more difficult to pay when younger people (who tend to be higher wage earners) elect to eschew the business of the church.

I, on the other hand, would answer that question with a qualified "yes" that does not in any way deny either the

right or the righteousness of every individual to choose his
or her own spiritual path. I have received the ultimate gift
of knowing that my beloved wife remains with me 24/7, and
yet the Church has as crucial a role to fill in my life today
as it did in my youth. Aside from representing (in theory if
not always in practice) a paragon of ethical behavior and
a sanctuary from the evils of this world, the Church mate-
rially helps the less fortunate of our global society while at
the same time serving as a vital platform for achieving and
honing spirituality. Without the Church and its teachings
that are rooted in the Bible, Torah, Koran, Vedas and other
holy works, true spirituality would be unattainable for many
humans. I am one whose body, mind, and spirit have been
transformed during these early stages of a spiritual journey,
and yet I find immense comfort and meaning in attending
any church service. If nothing else—and indeed, there is
a great deal more at stake—a church service provides the
ideal place and time for me to drop to my knees, clasp my
hands together, and express, either silently or aloud, my
eternal gratitude to God for the manifold blessings and
loves of my life, especially for the ultimate gift of my wife.

In addition, the inspiring words and beautiful hymns of
a church service feed the soul, and thus allow each of us
to pursue what I believe to be our primary purpose on this
earth: to grow spiritually during our tenure here before we
return home to where we all originated. Love—that is to
say, God—is the common thread that ties together all living
things and all religions in a rich tapestry that connects all
the dots in our universe. It is precisely this love that the
Church espouses, whatever its faith, despite the hatred and

evil so evident in this world, sometimes even in our own backyard. The best we as spiritual beings can do during our brief tenure on earth is to try our best to connect as many dots as possible, one dot at a time. That is precisely what Jesus Christ and other harbingers of Divine Will have instructed us to do.

Is not such a message worth heeding, respecting, and supporting, whatever its source?

⌒

As a footnote to the above, the transition from believing something is true to knowing it is true is related to the type of experiences an individual encounters in a lifetime. For example, believing in God and the promise of an afterlife comes about from a vicarious experience such as going to church on a regular basis or taking a religious class. One believes in God and life after death because she or he has been taught these truths, as Victoria and I were, and/ or because people we admire believe them. In such cases, belief is based on faith.

Coming to know these truths, however, results from an intensely personal experience such as a reading from a qualified medium who presents facts and data that are unknown to the medium and thus can only emanate from one possible source in the Universe; that is, from someone actually living in the spirit realm. In such cases, knowledge is based on hard evidence that is impossible to deny.

⌒

Although we as human beings cannot control the actions of others, we can control our own choices—each of which, large and small, has consequences that impact us and those around us. We, and we alone, are responsible for the choices we make during our lifetime and for the quality of the life we lead. It serves no purpose to blame others for our mistakes and misfortunes, or to throw a pity party for ourselves. Every individual on this earth has the power and the ability to change bad to good, and to bring peace, joy, and serenity into their life.

Since love is the soul's true nature, it is always better to make choices based on love rather than fear or anger. The soul's compass course in making life's decisions is grounded in intuition. The "gut feeling" we all experience from time to time tends to point to true north. If it doesn't feel right, it probably isn't. We must all learn to trust our intuition— which is to say we must learn to put our trust in love—else we are in danger of careening down a slippery slope into the dark side.

Yes, the spirit realm exists and is separated from us, the living, by what is often referred to as a "thin veil." In other words, heaven is all around us, invisible to us yet as "real" as the ground we walk on. We are all One with God, and the desire to communicate between the spiritual and physical realms is also real and goes both ways. But for that to happen, we of the physical realm must be open to the possibility of someone in the spirit realm trying to communicate with us. We therefore must be receptive to such communications. Who is to say how many such signs Pat Leavell may have missed from John—or how many signs I may have missed from Victoria—while we struggled through the various phases of grief? I imagine quite a few.

I also believe that those we love in the spirit realm pro-actively act with our spirit guides and do what they can to help us through difficult and challenging circumstances. In earlier chapters I profiled several examples of such assistance I have received. Further, I believe that sometimes a physical being has to ask for help from the spirit of a dearly beloved—or from God, the Great Spirit—for that help to be forthcoming.

For example, as I came close to finishing the writing of *Victoria: A Love Story*, I assembled a team of book-publishing professionals of my acquaintance who were ready, willing, and able to help me with the interior design, cover design, editing, and other critical elements of a quality publication. When the question arose of what font to use for the word "Victoria" on the cover, Cathy Helms, president of Avalon Graphics, asked me which design I preferred of eight possible designs she had created for my consideration. It was a difficult choice. All eight designs were superb. Several of them were quite simple in construction while others contained the ornate flairs and sweeps that Cathy thought might best reflect Victoria's artistic bent.

Although I was instinctively drawn to number 4, I could not articulate why. Then it hit me. The question was not the font that I preferred; rather, it was the font that Victoria preferred. For the first time ever, as I sat at my desk I closed my eyes, clasped my hands together as in prayer, and said aloud, "Dearheart, this is your book and I want it to be perfect for you. If you can, please send me a sign of what font you prefer for the title."

In truth, despite whatever progress I had made on my evolutionary journey toward spiritual awakening, I did not expect an answer. So I was intrigued when, several minutes later, the telephone rang. It was my oldest son, Churchill, calling to check in with me as he generally did two or three times per week. As we started chatting about a host of topics, another thought popped into my mind. Of my three sons, Churchill has inherited the lion's share of his mother's artistic genes. Even at an early age he was creative in everything he did—drawing a picture; building a house or pirate ship with Legos; or, in the winter, fashioning a majestic snow castle replete with multiple interior chambers. Each day when his mother was in the hospital, he drew a scene on a glossy board that was reminiscent of our life together as a family. These depictions brought enormous peace and joy to Victoria during her final weeks and days. The last picture he drew, of the five of us enjoying lunch together at Jordan Pond on Mount Desert Island in Maine—Victoria's favorite restaurant ever—still hangs in our kitchen.

If anyone could speak to Victoria's artistic preferences, it was her eldest son.

"Churchill," I said into the receiver, "I need to ask a favor. After we hang up, I will send you eight fonts that Mrs. Helms has sent me for the title of Mom's book. We have to choose one of them. Please take a look at them and let me know which one you think Mom would prefer."

Churchill readily agreed. A few minutes after we hung up and I had sent him the array of fonts as an email attachment, the phone rang again.

"Dad," he said, "it's number four. No doubt about it."

"That was my instinct too," I replied. "But I didn't understand why. How were you able to decide so quickly?"

A pause, then: "Dad, you realize that's Mom's signature, don't you?"

Well, I had seen Victoria's signature a thousand times, of course, but I had not made that connection. Obviously she had, or else she would not have planted the thought in our son's head to call me in response to my appeal to her, and then planted the thought in my head to ask him for his opinion. (See Appendix B for the cover image.)

∽

A final story, also of a personal nature. In chapter 9 I said that I have had two dreams in which I believe Victoria was trying to communicate with me and send me her messages of love. The second dream may have been less complex in plot than the first one, but it was no less vivid in my remembrance of every intricate detail.

In the dream, Victoria and I were dressed in our bathing suits and crossing a bridge I recognized immediately. It was the Powder Point Bridge, a half-mile-long wooden affair (one of the longest wooden bridges in the world) that connects the coastal town of Duxbury, Massachusetts, to Duxbury Beach, a six-mile-long barrier island that is an ideal location to spend a summer day at the seaside. In real life, before we started having children, Victoria and I drove

the ten miles south from Hingham several times to partake
of that delight, always with a picnic basket secured in the
backseat of our Ghia.

In the dream the scenery was starkly clear: the heavy,
dark-stained wooden planks of the bridge; the azure blue,
unruffled waters that reflected the sun's rays in a most
pleasing fashion; the low-lying sand dunes and clusters of
beach grass ahead; and beyond, the vast, deep blue expanse
of the Atlantic. While walking across the bridge, we greeted
fishermen out to catch flounder, and according to what we
glimpsed in buckets they had brought with them, they were
having some luck.

Halfway across, Victoria suddenly slipped off her sandals,
jumped up on the left railing, and dove into the water. Startled and not a little concerned, I dropped the picnic basket,
leapt to the railing, and searched to my right and left for a
ladder leading from the water up to the bridge. Seeing none,
I shook off my sandals and dove in after her.

When I surfaced, the salt stinging my eyes, Victoria was
treading water and smiling at me.

"Why did you do that?" I spluttered.

"Because I knew you'd come in after me," she said.

"Of course I came in after you," I countered. "But we can't
get back up on the bridge. We'll have to swim to shore."

Victoria's smile never left her face. "Then I suggest we
get started."

As people lined the railing of the bridge to watch us,
we sidestroked together toward Duxbury Beach. As we
approached it, Victoria began to tire and I put her hand on
my shoulder to help pull her along. When at last we felt the

sand beneath our toes, we stood up and waded through the final few feet of water onto dry land.

"We made it," I said with relief. Nearby stood a knot of onlookers, one of whom had kindly carried our picnic basket and discarded sandals to us.

Victoria embraced me. "We always do," she murmured into my ear, "whenever we're together."

Behind us, the onlookers broke into applause.

The dream ended there but the story does not. When Victoria and I lived in Hingham during the 1980s and 1990s, we had a close friend who lived near us. John still lives in the area and in recent years he and I have renewed our friendship compliments of Facebook. On Facebook he posts hundreds of images of various scenes in Boston, the South Shore, and Cape Cod, only a few of which I see since I normally go on Facebook only once or twice a day and only for a few minutes each time. Nevertheless, those images I do see I tend to "like" because they conjure up happy memories of years gone by.

Two days after my dream John posted a photograph of Powder Point Bridge on his Facebook newsfeed. When I saw it, I was not the least bit surprised. I simply nodded to myself and smiled. Along my spiritual journey I have come to accept synchronicity as a perfectly normal phenomenon.

It's wonderful how the Universe works, isn't it?

# *Afterword*

The following message from Sanaya was received by Suzanne on December 4, 2014. It was subsequently received by me (and by thousands of other people) on that day via an email blast sent from Suzanne in the same hour that my editor returned the manuscript of this book to me. Since this was yet another example of two events being "too coincidental to be accidental," I felt compelled to share this communication. Each of Sanaya's daily messages is beautiful, meaningful, and inspirational, and I have come to rely on them as a basis for daily reflection. Sanaya's message on this day goes to the heart of this book and provides the ideal ending.

*Why do some die young? The answer, if you truly want to understand it, requires that you understand the purpose of all Life. Life goes on in multiple dimensions, not just in the experience as human beings on Earth. All beings in all dimensions are extensions of the One Consciousness extending Itself for the experience . . . for the growth to be had. And so, all of life is about increasing one's capacity to Love, for that is the essence of this Force.*

*Why do some die young, and some die in middle age, and some die old? For the variety of learning opportunities that this variety offers. If all died at exactly one hundred years of age, this lack of variety would impede the growth opportunities. Does not much soul growth come from the uncertainty of when a soul will depart this physical experience? Does not much soul growth come from what you perceive as your greatest challenges?*

*Know that those who die young most definitely do go on. They go on learning and growing and loving in other realms whilst keeping up with your growth here on Earth. You are still together, for what Love has brought together, no physical absence can keep apart. You will be with them again in a similar dimension. At a soul level, you are together now, but for now, whilst you remain in human form, you are simply experiencing different growth opportunities.*

*Love. They brought more of it into this world and it continues on because of them.*

~

To better understand Sanaya and to receive daily messages of hope, comfort and joy from Higher Consciousness, please visit Suzanne's website; www.suzannegiesemann.com and her blog: www.SanayaSays.com.

As Suzanne writes on her site: "As 'Suzanne Giesemann,' I am unable to instantly express my limited mind with such beauty or insight. By surrendering to Higher Consciousness, however, I am able to attune to Sanaya and All That Is, and to share that loving energy with others."

Amen to that, Suzanne.

# Appendix A

## Recommended Reading List

The books profiled below represent a good sampling of ones I have read and can recommend on a personal basis. They provide comfort and healing for those wading through the swirling waters of grief, and insightful information for those seeking spiritual guidance and enlightenment

*Wolf's Message* by Suzanne Giesemann
(Waterside Productions, 2014)
"*Wolf's Message* is a masterpiece of intrigue. If you have ever wanted to read a book that validates immortality and communication with loved ones who have passed on, then read this book. It is an authentic portal to the other side."
—Caroline Myss, author of *Anatomy of the Spirit*

*Messages of Hope* by Suzanne Giesemann
(One Mind Books, 2011)
"I have had sessions with Suzanne and I genuinely respect and admire her skills. She will touch you from a God-realized place, so pay close attention." —Dr. Wayne W Dyer

*The Priest and the Medium* by Suzanne Giesemann
(Hay House, 2009)
"Suzanne Giesemann has produced a wonderful book, very
beautifully written, filled with emotion, inspiration, and joy
—I gobbled it up with many different emotions coming to
the surface of my being. This was one of the most enjoyable
books I've read in a long time—the life journeys of two talented people that is a real page-turner!"—Amazon Review

*Love Beyond Words* and *In the Silence* by Suzanne Giesemann (One Mind Books, 2011 and 2013, respectively)
Two collections of 365 days of inspiration from Spirit. Each
message is a paragon of healing, comfort, and infinite
wisdom.

*Forever Ours* by Janis Amatuzio, M.D.
(New World Library, 2010)
The author chose her line of work (forensic pathologist) in
part because it allowed her to help unravel the mystery of
each person's death. By listening and talking to the loved
ones of the deceased, she could offer them some sense of
closure. In the course of her work, she has heard extraordinary stories from grieving loved ones, patients near death,
police officers, clergy members, and colleagues—stories
of spiritual and otherworldly occurrences concerning the
transition between life and death.

*Love Never Dies: How to Reconnect and Make Peace with the
Deceased* by Dr. Jamie Turndorf (Hay House, 2014)
"*Love Never Dies* is an astonishing and refreshing story of

survival of consciousness. [Dr. Turndorf] clearly shows the many ways spirit can communicate through us and with animals and even objects. I could hardly put the book down, and I have read many of these types of books."
—Dave Campbell, Certified Windbridge Research Medium (WCRM)

*Answers about the Afterlife: A Private Investigator's 15-Year Research Unlocks the Mysteries of Life after Death* by Bob Olson (Building Bridges Press, 2014)
What happens when we die? This is one of humankind's most important and enduring questions. Answers about the Afterlife brings a fresh and exciting perspective to this ancient question. Bob Olson presents an impressive compilation of many lines of evidence that converge on the conclusion that the afterlife is, in a word, real." —Jeffrey Long, MD, author of the *New York Times* bestselling *Evidence of the Afterlife: The Science of Near-Death Experiences.*

*The Case for a Creator: A Journalist Investigates Scientific Evidence That Points toward God* by Lee Stobel (HarperCollins, 2009)
The author's road to atheism was paved by science . . . But, ironically, so was his later journey to God.

*Adventures of the Soul: Journeys through the Physical and Spiritual Dimensions* by James Van Praagh
"James Van Praagh is honest and sincere in his writing. Even nonbelievers will become believers. I highly recommend this book." —Amazon review

*Talking to Heaven: A Medium's Message of Life after Death* by James Van Praagh (Signet, 1999)
"Talking to Heaven has opened my eyes to my Spirit and my Guides, or Guardian Angles. Everything makes sense after reading James Van Praah's book." —Amazon review

*Living Originally: Ten Spiritual Practices to Transform Your Life* by Robert Brumer (Unity Books, 2013)
Robert Brumet explores how most of our perceived problems stem not from the world, but from a false sense of self. Living originally is the art of knowing the truth about who you are. Using the book's ten spiritual practices, you can rediscover your origin—your true self.

*Afterlife Communications; 16 Peoven Methods, 85 True Accounts* by Gary Schwartz et al, (Amazon Digital Services)
This book describes methods people are using today to communicate with loved ones who have passed away. The authors are acknowledged experts in afterlife communications who developed the methods, are using them consistently, and are teaching people how to use them.

*The Sacred Promise: How Science is Discovering Spirit's Collaboration with Us in Our Daily Lives* by Gary Schwartz (Atria Books, 2011)
Sacred Promise brings the reader into the laboratory of scientist Dr. Gary Schwartz, where he establishes the existence of Spirit by its own Willful Intent—a proof of concept for deceased spirits. The author takes readers on a personal journey into the world of angels and spirits and reveals their existence and desire to help.

*The Infinite Way* by Joel Goldsmith
(Acropolis Books, 2013—reissue)
"Joel Goldsmith is a national treasure. Every word he speaks
engages your heart and wakes up your soul. *The Infinite
Way* opens a path to enlightenment. It's a book you can
read over and over. And it will remain ever new!"
—Amazon review.

*A Parenthesis in Eternity* by Joel Goldsmith
(Acropolis Books, 2013—reissue)
Goldsmith explains the Circle of Eternity—the basis of his
approach to mysticism—and tells how to transcend the
"parenthesis" of our everyday lives that falls between birth
and death.

*How to Speak Unity: A Seeker's Guide to the Basic Concepts
and Terms that Define this Practical Spiritual Lifestyle* by
Temple Hayes (DeVorss & Company, 2011)
Unity believes that we are all individual and eternal expressions of God. Our essential nature is divine and therefore
inherently good. Our purpose is to express our divine
potential as realized and demonstrated by Jesus and other
master teachers. The more we awaken to our divine nature,
the more fully God manifests in and through our lives.

*Healing After Loss* by Martha W. Hackman
(William Morrow, 2009)
A book of daily meditations to help those suffering from the
loss of a loved one get through the grieving process.

# Appendix B

Cover image of *Victoria: A Love Story*